INVESTING FOR TEENS & YOUNG ADULTS

YOUR GUIDE TO ACHIEVING FINANCIAL FREEDOM
THROUGH MASTERING THE FUNDAMENTALS OF
SAVING, EARNING PASSIVE INCOME, STRATEGIC
INVESTING, AND GROWING YOUR MONEY

DEE LYNN

CONTENTS

INTRODUCTION

" *An investment in knowledge pays the best interest.*

— BENJAMIN FRANKLIN

Can I ask you a very important question? What do you want your life to look like when you are 30 or 40 years old? Do you want to be able to travel the world and see amazing sites? Maybe you want a huge house that all your family can fit in. What about having your own business so you can be your own boss? Maybe you haven't even thought about it.

You might think it is way into the future, and you don't have to think about it, but it comes at you faster than you would think. Regardless of what dreams you have for your future, you need a plan to get there. You need to know what steps you should take so you can have enough resources to live the life you want when you are older. The best way to get to that point is to start investing. How you invest your resources, time, energy, and money will determine where you end up in the future. The problem is that most people will leave school, and they will not have a clue about investing. This is why many people spend their entire 20s making decisions that they end up regretting later on in life.

Maybe you picked up this book because you don't want to end up like that. You want to learn about what you can do now to set yourself up for the future. Maybe you were thinking about how you can turn your dream life into a reality. If this is you, then you are way ahead of many people your age. In order to get to that place, you are going to need a plan, and that is where this book helps you.

Investing can seem like such a daunting subject because it's all numbers. I get it. The good news is that you don't even have to be good at math or school to start investing. You just need to be able to create an investment plan that's going to make sense for you. There are a few basic rules that are going to help you to create financial goals that you can reach.

Then you can build a long-term plan to increase your wealth and live the life you want.

Many teens and young adults are catching onto the idea of starting to invest early. They may not have the money they need to invest large amounts, but what they do have is the willpower to keep learning and keep planning. This is so important for their financial future, and you will notice that it's going to be important for yours as well. By the time you come to the end of this book, you will have an investment plan that you can build upon, and this will help put you ahead of your peers. You will be more knowledgeable and confident in your investment plan, and this can help you build the life you want.

I have personally been in the finance industry for many years, so I have seen the difference between people who invest in their teenage years and 20s versus those who invest much later. The difference is staggering. I am an accountant for a nonprofit organization, and I have three children who I hope will start investing as soon as possible. I make sure to teach them as many principles as possible, so they are fully prepared for the world when they are adults. This is also the type of information I want to pass on to you so you are equipped to build a life you are proud of.

Many teenagers and young adults don't start investing because they just don't know where to start. I'm going to let you in on a little secret: you started when you picked up this book. The information that you are going to learn is going to help you to make your investment plan and start making better financial decisions. You might not know it now, but this is going to change your life and how you see money.

1

HOW MUCH MONEY DO YOU WANT TO BE WORTH IN YOUR 30S?

The average net worth of Americans under the age of 35 is $76,300, with the median amount being $13,900 (Costa, 2023). Since the median is the midpoint of all the data collected, it means over half of these are under this mark. Many people might even have a negative number because they are in debt. I'm sure you don't want to be owing back money or living below the average when you are in your 30s.

Thirty can seem like a long way away when you are a teenager, but I promise it comes at you so fast. One day you are minding your own business and writing your final exams at school; the next, your neck is aching for a full week because you slept funny! This is why it is so important to start thinking about your future now. You will be able to plan and prepare so you can live the life of your dreams when you reach that point in life.

WHY YOU DON'T WANT TO WAIT TO START THINKING ABOUT YOUR FINANCIAL FUTURE

Most teenagers are concerned about prom and what they are going to do for summer vacation. There is nothing wrong with any of that. You should definitely enjoy living in the moment. However, it is also smart to start thinking about your future. You are in an amazing position because you have the time to start as early as possible. This will help you build the right habits so you can avoid getting yourself into some financial trouble as you get older.

Gives You Freedom to Pursue Dream Hobbies

Some teens and young adults are lucky to have parents who will pay for their hobbies, but many do not. You might be in school now, and your parents might be willing to pay for your music lessons, sports clubs, or whatever other hobbies you have, but this isn't going to last forever. In most cases, when you graduate, your parents are no longer willing to pay for these things. You now must give up something you love because you cannot fund it yourself. If you want to try out a new hobby, then you have to put it on hold for a long time until you have the money for it. This can really suck!

Hobbies and activities that bring you joy are important. It is a big part of who you are, and having the money to do them is a big thing. The thing I see with many people under the age of 25 is they simply do not have the resources to do things they enjoy. Their finances are all over the place, so they sit at home all weekend even though they want to be out doing something else. A hobby can be anything from working on a new skill, bettering yourself in some way, taking on a new activity, or even traveling. It is all about what you want to do with your time. Having your finances in order will allow you to do things on your own and make sure you can start enjoying your life as soon as possible.

Comfort of Being Able to Cover Unexpected Expenses

I would love to tell you that everything in life can be planned out, but that is not the case. I have been living adult life for quite some time now, and I can promise you the only constant in life is that unexpected things will pop up. This is to the horror of those who love to have things planned out perfectly. The good news is that we can plan for the unexpected, even if we do not know what they will be.

Making sure you have enough money in the bank for emergencies is going to give you a whole lot of peace in your life. You won't have to worry about things as much, and you will feel secure. The thing with unexpected expenses is that they often come with stress. It is usually something that is an emergency that needs to be paid for ASAP. This means you will have to deal with the actual emergency and the finances behind it. It is not a great space to be in. When these things pop up in life, at least the financial side of things won't be as big of a stress.

Helps You Avoid Living Paycheck-To-Paycheck

Unfortunately, in this day in age, most people are living paycheck-to-paycheck. This just means that they do not have any savings. It can be very stressful to live like this because you have to hope and pray that your money will stretch until the next paycheck, and you do not have room to do anything spontaneously. This is usually the result of not budgeting properly. When you are not able to see where your money is going, it becomes very difficult to manage it.

Easier Debt Management or Avoid it Completely

Debt can hold a lot of people back. When you are in debt, it means that you owe someone else money. This happens when you have large amounts of credit and loans. It is a lot easier to get into debt than you might think. Most people believe they can handle it, but then it gets out of hand quickly. Not all debt is bad; for example, you can take out a mortgage to purchase a property, and this can be considered a good type of debt because you are investing in property. With this being said, most of the debt people get into is bad debt, and it is the type that gets out of hand.

Many people say the reason they get into all this debt is because they just want to pay for their everyday expenses. Learning how to manage your finances well will help you completely avoid debt. When you don't know how to handle money, it can be very easy to spend more than you should.

Compound Interest!

Compound interest is an amazing tool to build wealth. You might have learned about interest in school, but let's do a quick refresher. Interest is like a percentage fee that a lender will put on the money they let others borrow. So, if your friend wants to borrow $10, in return, they will pay you back 10% interest each week. If they do not pay you back, they will continue to owe you more and more money. After the first week, they will owe you $11 in total. After the second week, it will be $12.1, and the third week will be $13.31. This will continue to grow until they pay you back.

When you invest your money, you are using this same principle. You deposit money into an investment account, and the financial provider will be able to use that money however they want to. In return, you will be gaining interest on your investment. The longer you leave your money in the account, the more interest you will earn. As you can see from the example, the money is starting to increase quickly because you are earning interest on top of interest. When you take advantage of compound interest, you will be able to make a lot more money from less just because you have time on your side.

More Room for Risk Before Your Obligations Start to Pile Up

Investing does come with risk, but risk and reward have an important relationship. Many people like to stay away from risk, but when it comes to investing, you do need to take some sort of risk. Investing is never a guarantee, and when you put your money into an investment account, there will always be a risk that it might not work out how you plan. With safer investments, the risk is smaller, but the potential increase will also be less. When you have time on your side, you are able to make riskier choices with your investments because if something were to go wrong, you have time to make your money back.

Let's say you are 20 when you first start investing. At this age, you have about 40 to 50 years before you retire. This is a lot of time for your investments to grow. If you choose a riskier investment and it doesn't pan out the way you want, you have a ton of time to fix the mistake and change your plan. If you start investing at the age of 50, you only have 10 to 15 years until retirement. Risky investments will carry more risk because if you were to lose out, you do not have the time to fix it. This means you have to be conservative with your investments.

Starting younger means that you give yourself more time to learn. You can make riskier choices because you do not have many obligations. No house, kids, and important bills mean that you can focus on learning about investing. When you do reach the age where you have all these responsibilities, you will be settled in your investing plan.

FIVE STEPS TO SETTING YOUR GOALS

Did you know that simply setting the right type of goals can dramatically increase the chances of you getting what you want? Most people have goals set up but struggle to actually reach them. When you learn how to set the right type of goals, you become the type of person that reaches them. You allow yourself to be successful.

There are five steps to doing this. The cool thing is that it is easy to remember. All you have to do is remember SMART. Each letter is a different step in the process. We will be going through each one and explaining it so it becomes easier to understand. You can apply SMART goals to all areas of your life and not just to your finances.

1: Be Specific

The first letter in SMART stands for specific. Most people think their goals are specific, but they really aren't. Imagine your goal being a destination, and if you are like most of us in the 21st century, you can't get anywhere without a GPS. I would be lost without Google Maps, literally! If I want to go to my friend's house in a different city, I can just put in the city's name, and the GPS will take me there. I will end up in the correct city, but that doesn't mean I am close to my friend's house. I would need to put in the exact address, so I end up in the right place and enjoy the time with my friend. Knowing the exact location also helps with planning because I can plot the shortest route and plan to leave at an appropriate time. All of this only happens when the destination is specific.

When you are setting goals for your finances, you need to know the exact destination so you can create a plan. Setting a goal like "I want to start saving" or "I want to learn how to manage my money" sets a general direction, but it is not specific enough. How do you work towards these goals? It is far too difficult and can lead you to feel demotivated. All these goals need is a little tweak, and they will be a whole lot more specific:

"I want to start saving" turns into *"I want to save for an overseas vacation after graduation."*

"I want to learn how to manage my money" turns into *"I want to create a budget every month and stick to it."*

Do you see the difference? The specific goals tell you exactly what the end goal is, and you can plan and take steps toward it. If you know you want to take a trip in two years, you can start researching the costs involved. Then you will know how much money you need and what you need to save each month in order to reach that goal. A specific goal helps you create a plan, and then the action steps are easier to take.

2: Make it Measurable

Measurable goes hand in hand with being specific. It is important to make sure you can measure your goals because it allows you to create a real plan and see how close you are to reaching the goal. All you need to do to change your goals into something measurable is to add a number to them. Instead of saying you are saving for something, put a number to it. Figure out the exact number you need and then break it down to set some short-term goals.

If you want to save $1000 in a year, you will be able to make a clear-cut plan to move toward this goal. You will need to save just over $80 every month or $20 per week. You now know exactly what you have to do and can create short-terms goals to help reach your long-term ones. You will also be able to track how close you are to reaching your goal and can change your plan if you feel you are falling short.

3: Choose Something Achievable/Attainable

It can be so easy to think you can achieve so much more than what is achievable. Parents always encourage us by saying we can achieve anything we put our minds to. There is some truth to this, but it pays to be realistic. Most people do not think they can achieve more than what is realistic. If you get caught in that trap, then you can end up feeling very demotivated if you do not get close to reaching your goals. That can lead you to stop setting goals altogether, which is a horrible place to be in.

One of the best ways to set an achievable goal is to look at where you are now. If you know you earn $100 a week from your part-time job, saving $350 a month is probably not realistic because you only have $50 to spend on the things you need each month. This is not achievable because you do not actually have the funds. A better way to set a savings goal is to look at how much you spend each month and then see what you can realistically cut back on. There will be some things you need to pay for and others that are more of a luxury. If you know what the necessities are, then you have a better idea of how much you have available to save. This way, you set a goal that is realistic, and you know you can reach it.

4: Keep it Realistic

Realistic just means that you will be able to reach your goal based on your current situation, time, and resources. You might be tempted to set a financial goal based on something you are hopeful for in the future. You might assume that your uncle will give you a huge amount of money for your birthday this year because he does it every year, but this is not a guarantee. He might have gone through some financial difficulty, or maybe he doesn't feel like being generous this year. If you set your goal on something you cannot control, the goal is not realistic. Just because something might happen does not mean it is realistic. Just like winning the lottery is possible, but you can't set your whole life up around winning the lottery.

5: Make it Time-Sensitive

Have you ever pulled an all-nighter to study for a test or finish up an assignment that was due the next day? Be honest, I think we have all been there. Maybe not all. I knew a girl in school who would always hand in her projects and assignments early because she had a rigid study schedule that she stuck to. If you are like her, how does it feel to be better than everyone? Joking! For the rest of us mere mortals, the deadline is what motivates us. We need to have a timeline; otherwise, we will probably never get anything done.

I know that most of us will never hand in any assignments or write exams if the time is not set. This principle is true for all our goals. We need to set a timeline for ourselves so we can reach them. Make sure that your timeline is realistic, so you don't stress yourself out trying to reach it. If your goal is going to take longer than a few months, make sure to create check-points with smaller goals in between. This will help you stay on track. For example, if you want to save $250 in six months, you would need to save $50 a month. Your focus will be on your monthly goal, and this will ensure by the due date you will have the money you need.

Goal Examples

Now you know how to set goals, it is time to pick the right goals. There are plenty of different goals you could have. This depends on what you want and what is going to be good for you. Your goals could literally be anything, so you don't have to feel limited to the suggestions here. With that being said, the goals mentioned are really good ones because it sets you up for the future and allows you to be financially healthy.

You also don't have to have all these goals at once. Rather pick one or two to focus on first, and once you have gotten the hang of them, you can add another one. This way, things will be a lot more manageable for you.

Emergency Fund

An emergency fund is one of the most important things you could have in your life, especially when you become an adult. An emergency fund is an amount you save for emergencies. An emergency is anything unexpected that pops up. You might not have many of these emergencies as a teenager, but they will soon come as you become an adult. Building the habit from now on will save you a lot of trouble down the line.

Ideally, your emergency fund should be three to six months of your expenses since this should be enough to cover most emergencies. It also gives you some wiggle room if you lose your job and need time to figure out what to do next. The reason an emergency fund is so important is that it helps you not to get into debt. If you do not have any money for an emergency, then you will have no choice but to take out a loan or use credit. This can really set you back on all your other financial goals.

Build Credit

Having a good credit score is essential as an adult. Your credit score is what tells financial service providers how likely you are to pay back a loan. If you are looking to buy a property or another big item, then having a good credit score will give you a great opportunity to do so.

Most types of credit are only available to adults who have jobs. However, there are a few options for teens as well. Do some research on credit cards for teenagers in your area. You will need your parents to help take out one, but it will count towards your credit score.

Save for College

One of the biggest expenses you might have in your life is college. People get into a lot of debt in order to study and further their education. Many people are still paying off their student debt well into their 30s and 40s. This holds them back from their other financial goals and might keep them in debt for most of their lives. The best way to avoid this is to take out as small of a student loan as possible. This means you will need to save up before going to college. You can start doing this at any age, the sooner, the better.

Buy a Car

A car is seen as a rite of passage for most teenagers and young adults. When we watch movies, we see an emotional scene where the main character turns 16, and the parents hand them the keys to their dream car. This would be awesome, but it is not realistic for most people. Lots of people have to buy themselves a car, and this is a huge expense. Perhaps your parents are willing to pay a portion for your car. If so, find out how much they are willing to contribute and then see how much you will need to buy the car you want. This will give you a clear-cut goal to save toward.

Start a Business

If you dream of starting your own business one day, you will need some money to get going. The type of business you want to start will determine how much money you will need. Take some time to plan out how much money resources will cost you for your business, and then make a goal to save what you need as soon as you can. You might even be able to start your business before you graduate high school or college.

Build Passive Wealth

A passive income is a great way to make money without consistently having to put in the effort. There are a lot of ways you can do this, so pick something that works well with your skills. Starting a blog, YouTube channel, or social media page could be a good source of passive income. Once you put out your content, it will continue to generate income if you have enough people engaging with it. Selling digital products is also a good option for a passive income.

BUILD YOUR INVESTMENT PLAN

The goal of the section is to help me to build your investment plan one step at a time. There will be one of these prompts or exercises at the end of every chapter. If you want to get the most out of this book, then take some time to pause and follow the prompts to build your own investment plan. This will help to solidify the information in your head because we all know that sometimes things are easy to forget when we don't put them into practice.

Since this chapter is all about goals, that is exactly where we are going to start. Rather than starting off with a long-term goal, let's start with something short-term. What is something you want in the next three months? This could be some new clothes, a new video game, or even buying a present for someone close to you. Once you have your goal in mind, go through the steps of setting SMART goals. Do this one by one until you've created a step-by-step guide for you to reach your goal.

Make sure you break it up into what you need to achieve each month and even each week. Put this into your calendar or your Notes app and tick it off as you finish off your smaller goal for the week of the month. You will notice how much more motivated you feel when you have a plan in motion for your goals. This is just to teach you how to set your goals and what you can do to reach them. Once you have got this down, you can move on to more long-term goals. That might be a bit more difficult to reach.

Writing down your goals is a very powerful act. It helps you to remember it, and you can think of it as a contract to yourself. Now you are committed to doing something, and it is tangible in the real world. Stick this goal somewhere you will see it each day. This will help you remember it and make the right choices each day so you can reach your goals.

When it comes to most of our financial goals, we can't simply store the cash under the mattress. We need to use a bank. For someone who has never used a bank before, it can seem a bit daunting. This is why we are going to go through banking basics in the next chapter so you can understand how to use it to help you reach your goals.

2

HOW TO BANK THE RIGHT WAY

No matter your age, people will feel differently about banks. Some people do not like them, and others have no problem with banks. It really helps when you fully understand banks and what they do. This will help you make better choices with your banking accounts so you can take full advantage of them.

WHAT EXACTLY DO BANKS DO?

Before getting into how to use banks, you need to know what they actually do. I am sure you have a general idea of what a bank is and how it works. For most people, they just deposit their money into a bank and call it a day. It can seem like a place to just keep your money for a fee. This is part of why banks exist, but, a bank is a middleman when it comes to finances.

The bank acts like a middleman for people looking to borrow and lend money. Some people go to the bank to borrow money in the form of loans, and others want to deposit their money as an investment or for saving. Have you ever wondered why banks have so much money to loan out to people? Well, the truth is that they use the money you deposit. Once you deposit money into a bank account, it doesn't just stay there. The bank uses it for its own purposes. This is especially so when you use a savings account and lock in your money for a certain amount of time. The interest you earn on your money is what the bank pays you for using your money. Crazy, right?

Banks can also take money entrusted to them and invest it. Then they can increase their funds and have more money to play with. Banks can use your money to make them more money as well. Some people think that because of this, banks are not safe, but in reality, they are probably the safest place to leave your money. Carrying cash around is not realistic. Tell me: Where would you hide a million dollars in your bedroom? Plus, you will never be able to earn interest that way. Banks are secure, but they do look to benefit from the services they provide to others. Banks play a very important role in the economy, and there are very strict regulations put in place to make sure everything runs well.

What Are the Main Roles/Functions of Banks

Banks have many different roles and functions beyond being a place to save your money. There are probably hundreds of products and services you can get from a bank. It is important to know the main ones so that you don't feel overwhelmed when you have to start your banking journey.

A bank is going to be your go-to place for most of your financial interactions. You can get a regular banking account which could be a checking, savings, or money market account. You would also be able to take out loans and credit cards. Your bank also might offer business banking and insurance services. It is always a good idea to do your research on the banks in your area so you can get the best bang for your buck. You also want to make sure your chosen bank is reputable.

Each service the bank offers you will come with a certain fee tied to it. As a student, you'll probably be able to get a bank account for a relatively low fee. It is a good idea to take advantage of this because the fees do increase as you start earning more money.

How a Bank Can Make Profit

Most people believe that the fee we pay in order to open a banking account is the main way a bank will make money. However, this is not usually true. The fees are a small amount of how banks make money but not the whole picture. Most banks will make money through various different avenues so they can increase the amount of revenue that comes into the bank. Banks are also businesses, so it is important for them to make a profit.

We have already spoken about the income that comes due to fees. The other type of income in a bank comes from interest. By taking the money that people deposit into the bank and loaning it out to people who need loans, a bank can make interest. The bank charges interest to those who take out the loans and pays back interest to those who have deposited money into the bank. You will notice that the interest on loans is higher than the interest that is gained through saving and depositing money into a bank. Different types of loans will have higher or lower interest fees. Interest rates also change over time, depending on the economy and many other factors. It is important to keep your eye on interest rates, so you know exactly what is going on in the banking industry and how you can profit from it.

Another way banks can make money is through capital market income. You can think of this as a marketplace where investors and businesses all come to connect with one another. An investor will have enough money to give to a business that needs it in order to grow and make higher amounts of profit. A bank acts as the facilitator between these two through trading services, underwriting, and M&A advisory. This gets into investing and the stock market. We will be talking more about all of this in later chapters.

Digital Vs. Traditional Banks

Almost anything you can find in the real world can also be found in a digital version. Except for petting zoos, I haven't seen a digital version of that yet, but who knows? Anyway, this means that you have traditional banks and digital banks. A traditional bank is one that can be found in a building. It is a physical bank you can go to and speak to a real person about your banking needs. A digital bank is one that operates completely online, and there are no physical branches for you to visit.

A digital bank cannot be considered a full-fledged bank because there are many restrictions imposed on them through banking licenses. Instead, they do banking as a service and offer multiple financial services just as a regular bank would. These types of banks have fewer expenses because they do not have to pay a large number of staff or pay for rent and other amenities for their banking premises. This means digital banks typically offer lower fees for the same services as traditional banks. You will also have mobile banking options, and you can manage your banking remotely from your phone or computer. This makes things a lot more convenient for the average person.

When it comes to traditional banking, it has been around for many years. Traditional banking has also moved into an online space since many of them do offer a few online banking features. With this being said, most physical banks rely on their branches to help you with your banking needs. The good news is that most traditional banks have buildings and branches all over the country, so you will likely find one close to you. You will also find ATMs located in common areas so you can access banking services and withdraw your money when needed. Traditional banks offer more services than digital banks, so depending on what you need, a traditional bank might be a better option for you. It is important to note that traditional banks come with higher fees since there are higher costs to operate one.

THE DIFFERENT TYPES OF BANK ACCOUNTS

When you go to open your very first banking account, you will likely be hit with a whole bunch of options. This can feel incredibly overwhelming if you do not know the different types of banking accounts out there. Each type of account will come with positives and negatives. Not every account will be suited for you and your needs, so it is important to understand all of them so you can pick the right one for you.

Checking Account

The checking account is the most well-known type of banking account. It is quite flexible, and it offers benefits to most people. A checking account can also be thought of as a transactional bank account. This just means that you will be able to spend money and have money deposited into this account. Most people will have their income deposited into this account, and their bills will be paid from here as well. This account makes it very easy to access your money quickly, so it's quite convenient for transacting.

If you have a checking account, you will also receive a debit card. You can use this card to swipe or scan for items at pay stations. This way, you do not have to draw out the cash if you do not want to. You will only be able to spend the money that is available in your account. If you try to buy something that is more expensive than the money you have in the account, the transaction will be declined. This is why it is important to keep track of how much money is in that account before you start swiping away.

Savings Account

Another common account is a savings account. This is where you will deposit money that you intend to save. Many savings accounts will have a higher interest rate than checking accounts. This means you can make more interest on the money you deposit into your savings account. It also separates the money that you want to spend and the money you want to save. It makes it a whole lot easier for you to save and prioritize doing it.

Many banks will allow you to open up multiple savings accounts. This is great if you want to separate your savings for specific things. Perhaps you are saving for a vacation. You could open a savings account just for this and deposit money into it. Then you might have a separate savings account for your car maintenance. And another for purchasing a new phone. Having them all separated is a good way to make sure that you are on track for all of your savings' goals. You'll just have to do your research to make sure that you are not paying additional fees for your savings accounts. It is also a good idea to understand if there are any minimum balances that need to be maintained with each account, as this can make it difficult to use.

Money Market Account

This can be thought of as a hybrid account where the benefits of a checking and savings account are found in one account. You can earn a slightly higher amount of interest on it, but you will still have access to your money if needed. If you have an emergency fund, this is a great place to keep it because you will have access to your money if there is an emergency, but it is also separate from your transactional or checking account.

Certificate of Deposit

This is a place where you can put your money to earn some interest. Your savings will be locked in, and you will be able to withdraw it when the maturity date arrives. There are multiple time frames that you can choose from, including 12 months all the way up to 5 to 10 years. If you want to withdraw money from this account, you'll have to pay a penalty fee. These fees can be incredibly expensive, so it deters most people from taking out their money.

This might sound like a great account to save your money in, but it doesn't allow for any wiggle room. You should only save your money in this type of account if you are absolutely positive that you do not need to access it. Another thing to consider is that these accounts offer quite low interest rates. You should be looking for an account that offers you an interest rate that is higher than the rate of inflation. Inflation is when all the prices of items increase by a certain percentage. Inflation is typically around 3% every year, so if your interest rate is lower than this, then you are basically losing money. Many certificates of deposit accounts offer you an interest rate of around 1% or slightly more. This means they are not usually worth it. Make sure to take these things into consideration if you do want to take out an account like this.

HOW TO CHOOSE A BANK

There are many banks to choose from, so if you are wondering where to even start, I've got you. You will need to consider quite a few things so you can make the best choice for you. You can't just pick the bank that your best friend has because they might have different needs than you do. You don't want to be paying a large amount of fees when you could be getting a better deal for the same number of benefits. Changing your bank can be incredibly tiresome, so people typically stick with one bank for a long time, even if it isn't the best choice. This is why it is much better to take some time to do your research and pick correctly from the get-go. It's going to make your life a whole lot easier down the line.

Pick the Right Account for Your Goals

Every person is going to have different financial goals. There are also various bank accounts that are suited for all these financial goals. Picking the right bank account for the goals you have is essential. Think about what you want to use your bank account for, and then see what options are available to you. If you want to save, then a savings account is going to be your best option. You can then research the different interest rates on various types of savings accounts so you can make the best choice. It is always best to shop around before you make a final decision.

Look at the Fees

The next thing you want to look at is the fee structure. Some banks offer a flat fee. We will pay once a month for all the services included. Other banks work on a fee-and-commission type of structure. This is where you will be charged a standard fee as well as additional amounts for services you'll be using throughout the month. This can actually be a good option if the fee is relatively low, and you know that you aren't going to be using any advanced services. It is always worth it to make sure you are not paying for things you will not be using.

Think About Convenience

You need to make sure the bank you choose is convenient for you. This means there needs to be ATMs close to you, and the actual branch should be easy to get to. Many people do not think about this before they sign up with a bank and then put off doing important things due to the bank being too far away. If you are using a digital bank, this will not be as much of a problem.

Consider Credit Unions

Depending on what you need from a financial service provider, you can also consider a credit union. This is a nontraditional way to bank because a credit union is owned by the members, and this means it is a nonprofit organization. The savings rates tend to be much higher while the fees are lower. You just have to check that you meet the requirements in order to join. This is not an option for everyone, but it is always a good idea to do some research and find out if it's going to work for you.

Study Digital Features

Being able to access your bank on the go is a great feature and something you should be looking into. It makes everything easier and more convenient. Most banks offer some digital features, but there are many that have not made the transition. Some banks have a mobile app that makes accessing your bank on your phone easier, and others require you to log in with your browser. Browser-run apps are not as efficient, which is something to think about. Make sure you know what is available to you digitally so you know if the most important things can be handled from the comfort of your home.

Look at Terms and Conditions

Most of us do not bother to read the terms and conditions these days. It has become just a little check box that holds us back from moving to the next step of whatever we are doing. I hate reading the terms and conditions as much as the next person, but when it comes to banking and your money, it is something you have to do. Take some time to sit down and go through the terms and conditions so you are not caught off guard. Signing a contract with the bank means that you are legally bound by it, and if you don't know what this entails, you might end up not getting the service you want. If you are confused about something, bring it up with the consultant opening your account and perhaps bring it up with your parents as well.

Read Reviews

Before I buy anything, I always look at the reviews. Why? Well, it shows me what a normal person thinks about the services or products they receive. It helps me to make a decision because I can see whether people are getting what they expect or if they feel cheated. The same should go for banks. Looking at the reviews will help you to understand whether the bank is going to give you the best service or not.

BUILD YOUR INVESTMENT PLAN

There are many different banks out there, and each one has its own positive and negative aspects. The great news is that it is super easy to find out more about these banks online. Take some time to write out a list of a few banks in your area that you might be interested in. Then write out a few pros and cons of each bank so you can decide which one is going to be the best fit for you. Remember to consider the fees you will be paying and what you will be getting in return for it. You can use the sheet below to help you do this, or you can create your own.

Bank name	Fees	Benefits	Other notes

Once you have chosen your bank account and you know that your money is going to be safe there, you can then move on to investing. Investing is the step when you get to grow your money so you can reach your goals a lot quicker. There are a lot of concepts to understand when it comes to investing. That's why we are going to go through all of these things in the next chapter.

3

THE BASICS OF INVESTING

Invest for the long haul. Don't get too greedy, and don't get too scared.

— SHELBY M.C. DAVIS

Investing is something that everyone should be doing regardless of age. Older people who have not thought of investing can have a hard time with it. This is why it is important to start as young as possible. It helps you to develop the habit and the courage to do it and keep going. Investing early also means you give your money more time to start working for you. You will be miles ahead of your peers by understanding investing as a teenager or young adult.

WHAT INVESTING ISN'T

With all the positive aspects and the amazing benefits that come with investing, some people have really misunderstood the concept. We now have hundreds of influencers and scammers who talk about investing in the wrong way. It gives people a bad idea of what investing is, and then people make bad decisions with their money. In this section, we're going to go over a few of the investing myths you should avoid when you start out on your investing journey.

Something Only the Wealthy Can Afford to Do

This myth is actually true...if we lived in the 1920s. Back in the day, investing was only something rich people could do. They used investing to grow the money they already had, and you needed to be rich in order to start. This means the average person could not invest their money and could not build wealth in this way. We do not live in those times anymore, and investing is a lot more accessible to everyone. This is why teenagers and young adults can start investing with very little money. You don't have to have thousands of dollars to get started. In fact, it is better to start with a little bit and build up the habit, so you know what you're doing when you have a lot of money. As you get older, you will be able to invest more money and invest in different options as well.

A Game of "Timing" the Market

Let me first explain what the market is. When people say that they are referring to the stock market. This is just a place where an investor can go and buy shares in different companies. The investment money is used by the company to expand the business and grow in order to bring in more revenue. When this happens, the investors get a profit out of this. So, you can buy a share in a small company for $5. We call it a share because it is a part of the company, so you basically have ownership of that part. This doesn't mean you can make any decisions; you have just financially partnered with the company. Let's say your $5 got you 1% of the company (this is not a realistic number, but we will use it for this example). The company can now use your money and the money of hundreds of other people who also invested. This allows them to hire more staff, build more products, and be more successful. They increase their profits and growth by 20% because of the investments. Your $5 is now worth $6 because of the growth, and the longer you leave it in the market, the more interest you can possibly make. There are tons of things that can affect the price of a stock in the market, so it is not always as clear-cut as this.

The stock market can be quite volatile. This means the prices will go up and down. The price of a stock or a share can increase or decrease in a matter of minutes. This makes people think that they need to time the market, so they purchase share or stock for a small price and sell it at a higher price. This strategy is really difficult to put in place, and it is not that effective. What is most important is the overall upward trend of a specific stock you have purchased. If you try and time the market, there is a higher chance of you not making as much profit as you would like, and it can be pretty stressful. The best way to invest is to choose your investments wisely and leave them to grow for a long period of time. The stock market has historically increased over time, so we can trust that this will continue to happen. Even if it looks like something is going wrong, leaving your money in your investments is going to be a much better option.

A Way to Get Rich Quick

Many people think the stock market is a get-rich-quick way to do things. There are definitely some people who have gotten rich fairly quickly through the stock market, but it is very rare for this to happen. Often, when people do get rich really quickly, they also get poor just as fast. Those who choose to use strategies that help them get rich quickly usually have to make it their full-time job, and it is a very small percentage where the strategy actually works. Do not believe the influencers who say this is the right way to go because it really isn't. You are going to have to put in a lot of effort and work, as well as do your research and be well-versed in the stock market to make this work for you. The effort you put in and the risk you are taking is simply not worth the potential reward. Not to mention the percentage of people who do get rich super quickly is very small. Investing is a long-term game, and if you want to play, you must be in it for the long haul.

Like Gambling at a Casino

There are a lot of negative people out there who are against investing in the stock market because they believe it is like gambling. When people talk about taking risks in order to get a big reward in the stock market, it can be easy to believe it is like gambling. There are definitely some similarities, but the way a casino works and the way the stock market works are vastly different. Firstly, gambling at a casino is designed to make gamblers lose. Casinos are in it for their own profit rather than the profit of the gamblers. With the stock market, it is mutually beneficial to investors and the owners of the stock. Investors put their money into certain companies, and the companies can use that money to build up and grow; this generates more profit for the investor.

The other big difference is that the more time you spend in the stock market, the more beneficial it is for you. This is not the same with a casino. Historically the stock market has increased over the past few decades. With casinos, those who gamble for a long amount of time tend to lose more money. These are all important aspects for you to remember when confronted with the idea that gambling and investing are the same thing.

A Risky Way to Make Money

When you start investing, you will often hear the term "risk." This can scare people away because they don't want to make a risky move with their money. The reason risk is involved with investing is that you can never be 100% sure an investment will pan out. That is simply the nature of investing. Think about it this way, if you were to start a company and had a brilliant idea that you knew people would want to buy into, you would need to go to an investor and ask them to invest in your idea so you can start your company. You would show this investor all the potential profit and benefits they could get when your company is up and running. Even if you have the best idea in the world, there will always be a risk that your company might not get off the ground or might not make the amount of profit you think it would. The investor is going to be taking a risk in investing in your business.

After running all the numbers and checking out the statistics, you would say there is a 90% chance that your business will be successful. This is high odds, and most investors would probably be interested in looking into your business as an investment. However, there is still a 10% chance that your business could tank. Perhaps there is a global pandemic (flashback to 2020), and you can't get the resources you need. This means whatever money the investor has given will be lost. An investor will only get money if your business is profitable. They will get a percentage of those profits. The investor is making a potential risk now, so that in the future, they can profit from it and hopefully for the rest of their life.

This is the basic idea of the stock market and risk. Even if the risk is small, it is still there. Sometimes we take more risks to enable ourselves to get more reward. This doesn't mean that we have to make dumb choices. We always have to do our research and make sure the investments are sound. However, it is always important to remember that there will always be a small amount of risk when it comes to investing, but that doesn't mean that investing is risky. In fact, it is one of the best ways to grow your money.

Better Left to Finance Professionals

Back in the day, you had to be a finance professional in order to invest because it wasn't something accessible to the average person. Not only that, it seemed incredibly complicated, so most people simply didn't do it. These days there are lots of measures in place to make sure that the average person can invest and grow their wealth. We also have ways to invest that are very low maintenance, so you don't have to be a finance guru in order to do it. We will talk more about the different ways you can invest, and you will be able to understand why you don't have to have a masters in finance to get going.

Something to Think About When You're Older

People typically wait to invest until they are much older. This is one of the biggest mistakes that you can make because the longer you have an investment, the more opportunity it has to grow. You can take a small amount of money and grow it into a much larger amount over time, but you need to give it that time.

When you are younger, you can make slightly risky investments because you have more time to recover if something bad were to happen. This is great news. If you are a teenager or a young adult who is looking to invest, just get started and do your best to grow your money. You don't have to be in your 40s to start investing.

WHAT INVESTING REALLY IS

Now that we have debunked most of the myths that surround investing, we need to start talking about what investing really is. It is super important to understand the basic concepts of investing. Otherwise, you will get caught up in myths and lies that surround the industry.

Many teenagers and young adults find it difficult to fully understand what investing is and how it works. It can seem like a very complicated topic, and it's the reason why so many people will just avoid it altogether. Investing simply means that you are putting your money into something that will be able to give you a profit in the future. You are basically increasing your money. Investing can take many forms, so it is not a one size fits all thing. Each person needs to decide what they want to invest in and what's going to be best for their lifestyle and resources.

Investing is not the same thing as saving your money in a traditional savings account. When you save your money, the goal is to make sure you are saving the exact amount you need. This is usually for your short-term goals. For example, you could be saving your money for a new pair of sneakers. You know how much the sneakers cost and will save that exact amount until you have enough to buy them. The goal of investing is to build long-term wealth. This might not be for a specific goal in the future, but you want to be able to grow your money so that you have enough to take care of yourself when you retire or for other long-term goals.

There are two ways investments can help make you money. These are called appreciation and income generation. Appreciation is when the value of an item goes up over time. For example, property is an appreciation item. This is why we call it an asset. If you buy a house today, it will cost more in 10 to 30 years. If you sell the property, then you will be making more money than when you bought it, in most cases. This means your overall net worth goes up when you own a property. Income generation is when you can use your investment to consistently bring in an income. We can use property as an example for this as well. If you purchase a property and rent it out, it will generate money for you each month. You can use the money you charge for rent to pay off the mortgage on your property and have a bit left over for profit. Property has the ability to make you money in both investment avenues.

KEY INVESTING TERMS TO KNOW

Asset Allocation: This refers to spreading your investment capital amongst various kinds of assets. This helps to balance out the risk and gives you a better shot at making the most money through investing.

Assets: Something that has future value or value in the present.

Capital Gains: The money an investor makes after selling an investment for more than what they paid for it.

Compound Interest: This is the interest that is earned on the amount deposited or invested, as well as the interest earned on that. It helps an investment grow exceptionally quickly over time.

Interest: This is the percentage fee that needs to be paid in order to borrow money. This can go both ways in favor of the borrower or lender.

Margin of Safety: This helps to provide room for error when investing. A 50% margin is safe, so that means you invest half of what is the original price.

Portfolio: The total collection of investments that an investor has.

Return on Investment: The amount you can possibly get back on your investments. This helps you to figure out whether the investments are going to be worth it based on past performance.

Securities: A security is an investment instrument that is tradeable due to the fact that they will have the same value as each other.

Stock Market/Exchange: The place where buyers and sellers of stocks meet and conduct their business. This happens completely online in most cases.

Yield: This is a percentage amount that shows how much an investment has earned in a specific period of time:

BUILD YOUR INVESTMENT PLAN

Investing is going to be very personal to you. You won't be able to follow exactly what your parents did or what your friends are doing. You also should never copy and paste an influencer's strategy or a strategy from any person online. You never know the full picture when it comes to these things, and you might end up in a worse position for it. Since investing is so personal, you need to make sure you understand why you are doing it. Take some time to think about three personal reasons why you should be investing and how you should be investing. This could be tied to your financial goals and how you are going to reach them. If you are stuck on your financial goals, take some time and go back to Chapter 1 to revisit the information there. Remember that your financial goals can change, and so can your investment plan. Don't feel too much pressure to get everything perfect just yet. The main goal is that you are taking action toward building your investment plan.

Once you understand the basics of investing and why you actually want to start investing, you can start considering the different types of investments out there. The great thing about investing is that it can be completely personalized to you and what you need. There are so many different options out there, and this helps you create something specific to you. We are going to be talking more about this in the next chapter.

4

WHICH OF THESE INVESTMENTS DO YOU KNOW?

> *What's comfortable is not the right way to invest. You must own things that you're uncomfortable with. Otherwise, you're not really diversified.*
>
> — PETER BERNSTEIN

THE DIFFERENT TYPES OF INVESTMENTS

There are so many different types of investments that you can make. You don't have to utilize all investment types since this can be overwhelming and might be too difficult for you to track. Start with one or two investments, and then build up your portfolio from there.

Stocks

The first type of investment is definitely one of the most popular types. This is a stock. We have already spoken about stocks and briefly discussed how they work, so you should have a basic idea. In order to invest in stocks, you will need to go through a broker and use the stock exchange. This is where you trade your money for portions of a company. As the company grows and brings in more profit, you will be compensated accordingly.

In most cases, it is best to purchase your stocks and leave them to grow for as long as possible. If you have chosen well, you can almost guarantee your stock portfolio will increase over time. Some people do something called day trading, where they buy and sell their stocks within the same day. This allows them to make money daily, but it's also a riskier way of investing. You must be very quick when you are day trading since the prices fluctuate so fast. Most people who day trade will do this as a full-time job rather than a passive form of investing. You will also need to make sure you are doing a ton of research so you can invest in the right stocks.

Bonds

A bond is another very popular way to invest. It is much safer and more stable than stocks. It is usually a good idea to have a mixture of stocks and bonds in your investment portfolio. Bonds do grow much slower than stocks, but that is because they are a safer option. When you purchase a bond, you are basically loaning money to a specific entity or the government. You will then collect interest on the money you are leading to the specific entity. This is a stable growth, and once your bond matures, you will be able to take out all your profit, as well as the principal amount you invested at first.

Mutual Funds

A mutual fund is a great way to invest because there is a mixture of different kinds of investments, all under one umbrella. You will need to buy into a mutual fund through a financial service provider, and a manager will be assigned to your portfolio. The fund manager will pull multiple investors' money together and invest in various areas. This means there is more money being invested and, therefore, a better likelihood that there will be a good return. The profits are then split among all the investors equally, depending on how much they are paying into the fund. This type of mutual fund is called an actively managed fund because there is somebody constantly making decisions on what should be invested in. You will be able to find out where your money is going and make requests if you speak to the fund manager. This is definitely a great way to invest if you are a beginner because there is not much work that needs to be done on your part. You will have to agree on a certain amount that you will be paying each month that can be invested for you.

There is also a passively managed fund, which is typically called an index fund. This doesn't have a fund manager who is making the decisions. Instead, it tracks the stock market. Based on the results of the tracking, your money will be invested accordingly. Regardless of the type of mutual fund you are investing in, it does come with a fee. This is because you need to pay for a specific service that you are receiving. You can shop around and see what your options are in this regard. Make sure you're not being overcharged on your fee, as you want to make sure most of your money is going toward your investments.

Exchange-Traded Funds (ETFs)

This is very similar to a mutual fund in terms of having multiple different investments under one umbrella. The major difference is that you can buy and sell your ETFs on a stock market exchange. Instead of trading one stock individually, you'll be treating it as a package deal. It is like having a diversified investment portfolio but just in the stock market. It is a good option for beginners as you don't have to worry about investing in individual stocks and carrying out the risk like this. There is less risk involved in an ETF because there are multiple different stocks in one.

Options

It is a good idea to understand what an option is, but it is typically not the best choice for a beginner investor. It can be very complicated and difficult to get started with. With this being said, many people enjoy using options as a good way to diversify their portfolio after they have made other types of investments. When you buy an option, you are essentially buying the ability or option to buy or sell your investment at a set price at a future time. You can think of it as locking in a stock price now, but you're not paying anything or getting returns on that. The only time you will see the benefits of this is when you actually purchase the stock. The goal of doing this is if the price of the stock increases in value, you would've locked in a much lower price and can make a profit from that. It is definitely a risky move because there is also a chance that the stock will decrease in price, and you will have to pay more for a lower-priced stock.

If you are looking into this type of investment, it will take a lot of research, and you need to be well-versed in the stock market. If you have never invested in the stock market before, then it is a good idea to do simple investing techniques first. This way, you can fully understand how the stock market works and can better plan and prepare for options investing. Investing in options should not be your number one type of investing, and also not your only type of investing.

Annuities

Annuities are a great investment platform for retirement savings. You are basically investing in an insurance policy where you can get payments in periodic time intervals, but these payments only happen much later down the line. This means you'll only see benefits from an annuity in a few years and won't be able to take out any money now. There are various ways an annuity can work, and this all depends on the service provider who is offering it. If you choose to invest in annuities, it is a good idea to speak to your financial service provider and make sure you understand the terms and conditions. You should also weigh your options and compare the different types, so you are getting the best deal at the end of the day.

Certificates of Deposits

Out of all the investment types, a certificate of deposit is a pretty low-risk option. You will be investing your money in a bank and will need to leave it there for a certain amount of time that is predetermined. During this time, you are not allowed to take out the money, and you will be earning interest on it. Once the predetermined time has elapsed, you will get your principal investment back, as well as the interest, based on the rate agreed upon. The longer you leave your money in this kind of investment, the more interest you earn, and the more you will get back.

THREE SIMPLE STEPS FOR PICKING THE RIGHT INVESTMENT FOR YOU

Now, we are at the point where we have to pick the investments that are right for you. Every investor is different, and that means the strategy you use will be different from your friend. One of the biggest mistakes an investor can make is to try and copy someone else's investment strategy. If you don't have the right personality for a certain type of investment strategy, then you are likely not going to be successful with it. This comes down to a few key factors which we are going to be talking about in the section.

Think About Your Goals

The first thing that you should be thinking about is your investment goals. Each person is going to have different investment goals, and this depends on personality, values, and even your age. At the age of 18, you will have very different financial goals than when you are 50. It is totally okay for your financial goals to change throughout your life, but you do need to make sure you understand what they are at each point. Feel free to reevaluate your goals every so often so you can make sure you are always on track.

Let's say your goal is to build up a good amount of money for your retirement. You know that you don't want to work when you retire, and you want to enjoy those years by traveling and doing things you probably couldn't while you were working. In this case, you would probably need to take a bit more risk so you can allow your money to grow quickly. Since you're still young, you have enough time to take those risks and make sure your money grows to its highest potential. With this being said, you probably don't want to invest all of your money into risky investments. Otherwise, you could risk losing everything. At this age, you could probably start with 80% risky investments and 20% safer choices. Every 10 years or so, you can reevaluate your investment choices and choose safer options at a larger percentage.

Another goal you might have is to use your investments as a source of income. Not all investments will be able to give you a steady income, so you will need to make sure to choose the ones that help you reach this goal. A dividend stock is a type of investment that can bring you a passive income because it works slightly differently than a regular stock. With a dividend stock, you will be paid a certain amount from the profit or growth of the company. These payments are given at regular intervals and should be made known to you before you start investing. Sometimes this is quarterly (every three months) or even annually, depending.

You might also want to consider something like real estate if you want to make an income from your investments. Bear in mind that you will need a good amount of money to start real estate investing. Even if you do take out a mortgage, you will need to pay a deposit when you buy a property. This is a percentage of the total amount of the property. The larger your deposit, the lower your monthly mortgage payment will be. This is definitely a bonus and helps make things more manageable. Taking on a property is not a small task, so make sure you do your research before making this kind of investment. Many young adults will buy property because they think it is the right thing to do, only to find out there are tons of hidden costs that they weren't prepared for. Maintenance, property tax, homeowners' association (HOA) fees, and many other things become your responsibility when you own your own property. If you are not prepared for this, then you might end up in a worse financial position. This is not to scare you away from property. It is definitely a great asset to have; just make sure you are ready for the responsibility.

Figure Out How Much Risk You're Willing to Take

Let's talk about risk really quick. There are some people who are natural risk-takers; those tend to be the people who always find themselves in the principal's office at school. Then there are others who like to play it safe. There is actually nothing wrong with being a risk taker or someone who plays it safe, but you do need to know where you sit on the scale. Risk for someone who is not a risk taker can make them feel very nervous, and then they start to obsess about their investments. On top of that, it can be very stressful, and then they are not going to enjoy investing. Investing can be very emotional because you are using your hard-earned money for it. If you are not someone who can handle it, then be honest with yourself; otherwise, you aren't going to enjoy it.

Age plays a huge factor when it comes to risk. Let's say you are 20 years old right now and are going to retire at 70. This means you have 50 years to invest before you need to take your money out. Because your goal is so far away, you can take on more risky investments. If you are 60 right now, you will need to be a lot more conservative with your investments because if something were to happen, you don't have a lot of time to fix it.

Another factor that can come into play with risk is how much money you have. Someone with a lot of money to invest will be able to take on more risk because they have lots to spare. Someone who has a little will need to play it safer because it will be a huge setback if their investments do not work out. When you are much younger, this is less of a consideration, but as you get older, you will need to understand how the amount of money you have plays a role in how risky you can be.

Consider Your Portfolio Mix

It doesn't matter whether you are someone who is taking a lot of risk or someone who is playing it safe; we will all need to consider our portfolio mix. Your investment portfolio includes all your investments, and it is your job to make sure it is balanced. A well-balanced portfolio will allow for some risk, so you have the opportunity to grow your money quickly, as well as be stable enough to carry that risk with investments on the safe side.

Things like property and bonds tend to be on the safer side of investments. They will grow slower, but you can be secure in the fact that your investments are likely to work out. Growth stocks tend to be a lot riskier even though they have the ability to make you the most money. You can look at your investment portfolio like a pie or a pizza. It will be cut up into different sections, and it is your job to decide how many slices each investment type will get. As you get older, you will re-balance your portfolio based on your needs and what is going on in your life. This might mean taking away a few slices from the high-risk category and putting them into a lower-risk investment. The best type of invest-ment portfolio is going to be one that is diversified and has multiple different types of investments in it. You always want to have some level of risk and some level of safety in your investments.

BUILD YOUR INVESTMENT PLAN

Take some time and go through the list of investments that we have spoken about. Then pick two or three that you think would be the best fit for you. Write down these options and highlight a few reasons why you think these are going to be the best options. Do some additional research online to find out how you can invest in these options. Then start looking into what you need in order to start investing. If you are still a teenager, you will need the assistance of a parent or guardian to help set up your investing avenues.

On top of knowing where to invest your money, you also need to have a strategy to help you make the best choices. There are plenty of investment strategies out there, and it is up to you to develop one that's going to work the best for you. Since there have been many investors that have come before you, you can get a general idea of what an investment strategy looks like. In the next chapter, we are going to be diving into different types of investment strategies to help you make your choice.

5

HOW NOT TO GAMBLE YOUR MONEY AWAY ON INVESTMENTS

I nvesting is actually pretty easy. It's the making money part that comes with complications. You see, technically, investing is just putting your money into something and hoping for a better return. However, if you don't have a good strategy, things might not always work out how you want them to. You want to avoid this happening because we all want the best for our money.

THE BEST INVESTMENT STRATEGIES FOR YOUNG ADULTS

The best investment strategy for you will be the one that makes you the most amount of income with the least amount of stress. When it comes to investment strategies, you need to have one before you actually get going. Your investment strategy will probably change throughout your life as you learn more about yourself and about investing as a whole. This doesn't mean you can go in completely blind without a plan from the beginning. Having some sort of plan will allow you to see what works for you and what doesn't. It gives you a little bit of structure, so you're not completely lost in the process. Some people believe investing is all about luck, but this is not the case. The most successful investors are always the ones who have thought about the plans and then do their best to implement them properly. It is always best to follow in these people's footsteps rather than the footsteps of the people who wing it.

Four Basic Investment Strategies for Beginners

There are probably hundreds of different types of investment strategies and patterns out there. The four we are going to be talking about form the basis of most of them, so you can build your investment strategy around these ideas. As you read through these different investment strategies, think about how you can apply them to your own life and whether it's going to work or not. Don't feel bad if something doesn't sound right or you think it's not going to work. Remember, every person is completely different, so it only makes sense that your investment strategy will also be different.

Value Investing

Value investing is a type of stock market investing where you look at the current value of the stock and make a prediction on what the intrinsic value of it is. There are many times in the stock market when a stock will have a value set on it that is less than what it actually is. Let me use an example to help explain this a bit better. Let's pretend that the stock market is a store. At the store, the workers will put a sticker on each one of the items to tell you how much it costs right now. Let's also say that the stocks you want to purchase are found in the candy aisle. You look down, and you see the sticker on your favorite candy bar is priced much lower than what you believe it should be or what it usually is. Because you love this candy bar, you know a lot about it, and you know the real price of it is probably not what the sticker is saying right now. This gives you the opportunity to buy the candy bar at a low price, so you'll be able to sell it at a higher price later on. You can almost be certain that you will be able to sell it at this higher price because you know the intrinsic value is higher than what is shown right now.

This is the basic principle of value investing. You will be looking for stocks that are undervalued so that you will be able to make a profit on them later. There are many reasons for a stock to show a lower value, and it is quite common. Sometimes it could be something happening in the market, or it could even be a fluke. Value investors know the real value of the stock they want to buy and notice when things dip below the intrinsic value. This is the basis of making decisions in the stock market when you use the strategy.

If you are going to use the strategy, you need to make sure that you are doing all your research. This will help you make an educated guess and ensure that you get the best possible outcome from it. The research you need to do is not only limited to the company you wish to purchase stocks from but also to the general industry. All companies on the stock market are going to fall under certain industries. This could be healthcare, technology, finance, and a whole lot of other options. Whatever happens to the industry as a whole can affect an individual company and an individual stock.

Growth Investing

This type of investment strategy is focused on the overall growth of your investment portfolio. Many investors who choose this type of strategy will be investing in funds and stocks that have the potential to grow in future years. They will put in a set amount each month to grow their investments through interest and the growth of the stock market.

Something to consider when you invest this way is that you are likely not going to have many opportunities to invest in companies that give out dividends. A company that is in a growth mode is going to be focused on using most of its finances to grow the business. Dividends are not going to be the number one interest at this point, so you will likely not have too much of an opportunity to get these dividends. With this knowledge, it is more likely that newer companies would be in the growth phase rather than fully established ones. Investors will be able to get in at a lower price and allow the company to grow over time and profit from this. It is slightly riskier due to the fact that you will likely be investing in newer companies. This is why doing your research is going to be so important, so you can fully understand what you're putting your money into and what the potential benefit of that is.

Growth investing is definitely not for everyone because it is a risky strategy to move forward with. However, it does have great potential to bring in a lot of money if you choose the right stocks. You also have to consider that this type of investment strategy typically thrives under specific conditions in the economy. There will be a point in time with a growth strategy that is just not going to work. For example, if there is a major recession and the economy is taking a hit, it might be very difficult to find companies that are growing at a rate good enough to invest in. In general, growth investing is not as stable as value investing, but there are definitely periods of time when investors can profit from this strategy. You will just need to make sure you understand when these pockets of time are so you can capitalize on them.

Momentum Investing

This type of strategy is when you look at the stock market and see what is currently growing and choose to invest there. Other strategies might look at intrinsic value and not consider the fact that the current price of the stock is quite low. Another name for this type of strategy could be riding the wave. If a stock has already been increasing over a certain period of time, these investors would like to ride the wave and consider it a good stock to invest in. In many cases, a stock would continue to grow over a period of time, and it's an indication of this being a good investment. A stock that is dropping in price is not going to be a good choice for the strategy as it shows that it is not stable and will not bring profit.

If you're looking to invest in this way, you will need the help of a technical analyst because the best way to make decisions is through data. Using data from previous months and years, an analyst can give you a better indication of how a stock may perform and whether it would be one that has momentum or one that is dropping. If you choose this type of investment strategy, you will need to be always on the ball. This means that you need to be able to buy and sell at a moment's notice because things can change so quickly. A profit turnover is a lot quicker with this strategy because you are buying and selling all the time. This means that it's not suitable for somebody who wants to make a passive income through their investing or somebody that simply does not have the time to keep buying and selling throughout the day or the month. It is typically not the best strategy for someone who is beginning to invest because it can be a bit complicated. Focusing on learning how the stock market works and the basics surrounding it should be what a new investor focuses on. If you do want to consider this type of investment strategy, you can do your research in the meantime, so when you are slightly more experienced in a few months or years, you can start implementing the strategy.

Dollar-Cost Averaging

With this type of strategy, you will be making investments into the stock market over the course of time, and you can do it while including other strategies in your overall investment strategy. All you have to do with this type of strategy is to decide how much you are willing to invest and invest it into an account each month. This can also be done automatically by setting up transfers from your bank. This means you don't even have to do anything, and your money will be invested where you want it to be. You don't have to constantly think about the strategies you need to employ because everything has been planned out in advance. When it comes to investing, the main priority should be to actually put your money into the investment. Doing this consistently over time means that you are going to see a benefit from it. You can use various types of investment funds to help you invest and do so automatically.

This is a great strategy for most investors because of its low commitment level. A fund manager will be able to do most of the work for you as long as you commit to depositing a certain amount every month. Many investors get stuck in the mindset that they are scared to invest because they don't want to include any losses. When you use this strategy, you don't really have to worry about these things because you will likely not see the losses right in front of you. Even if they are happening, your main goal is to look at the overall growth of your portfolio, and you don't have to get into the nitty-gritty of investing. It is still a good idea to learn as much as you can about investing, even if you choose the strategy. You still have some control over what is going on with your investments, and you can choose to add different strategies to your overarching investment strategy.

Which Investment Strategy Is Right for You?

There are three main things you should consider when you are deciding whether an investment strategy is the right one for you. It is important to look at all three before you decide so that you can get the best idea of what will suit you. Remember that you can always change your investment strategy at another point in life when things change for you.

Risk Tolerance

We have already spoken extensively about risk tolerance, so I'm pretty sure you have a good idea of what it is. You simply have to decide how much risk you are willing to take for a potential benefit in your investment. Remember that higher risk will likely mean a higher reward, but it could also mean a higher loss. Make sure you choose something that you're comfortable with rather than just chasing after money with no other reasoning behind it.

Expected Returns

If you have set up your financial goals, you will have a timeline of when you want to reach them. This will help you figure out how much you will need in order to reach your goals and how long you have to get there. With this information, you can discover whether certain investments are actually going to be worthwhile. If you aren't going to get the returns you want in the timeframe you need, it might not be the best investment option for you.

Effort Needed

This factor is incredibly important, and I don't think a lot of people actually think about it. It can be so easy to get caught up in the money side of things that you never think about what you actually need to do to grow an investment. Some investments need you to be fully involved in order for you to increase your earnings, and others are more passive. There are some people out there who love to be very involved with their investments, and other people who prefer to just let it sit and do its thing. You need to decide which type of person you are so you can choose an investment that is in the effort bracket you are comfortable with.

If you choose an investment strategy that requires a lot of work from you, but you simply don't have the time to do it, then you are never going to invest. You'll keep putting it off because doing the work just seems unappealing to you. There's absolutely nothing wrong with wanting to be a hands-off investor. If you don't want to be that involved, you really don't have to be. It's always best to look at yourself and decide what is the best action to take. Maybe in the future, you will have more time or energy to give into your investment, and then, at that point, you can change your strategy.

BUILD YOUR INVESTMENT PLAN

For this step in your investment plan, go through the different investment strategies and see which one is going to be best suited for you. It can be very easy to get caught up in thinking about how to make the most money, and you completely ignore every other part of investing. Every part of your investment strategy needs to work for you so that you can be consistent with your investing. Consistency is what is going to give you the best results over time, so be realistic with what you can do.

Investing is definitely something that rich people do to keep them rich. They know a few tips and tricks that most other people do not, and that is why they are able to keep and grow their wealth. In the next chapter, we are going to go over a few things that the rich do that we can also implement so we can be part of that 20%.

SHARE THE NEWS WITH OTHER TEENS AND YOUNG ADULTS: THE TIME TO START BUILDING WEALTH IS RIGHT NOW!

"If everyone is moving forward together, then success takes care of itself."

— HENRY FORD

Remember in Chapter 3, when we mentioned that investing is not something that only wealthy people can afford to do? We talked about the freedom that earning a passive income could bring you, much earlier in life than you ever expected.

Imagine being able to travel to places on your bucket list, having time to dedicate yourself to your personal passions, and enjoying quality time with the people you love—all within the next 10 years.

The media often sells you the idea that you have to work hard in your 20s and 30s and that you won't enjoy economic stability until you are in your 40s—but it doesn't have to be that way.

Many young investors have freed themselves of college debt before they turn 30, and that means they have the freedom to invest more money and make a killing through strategies like flipping real estate and earning compound interest.

You may wonder why investment isn't part of the educational system. Certainly, if you knew the ground-breaking difference it makes in your life, you would have started earlier.

Take a look around you, and you will find many young investment trailblazers—people like Alex Banayan, who became a venture capital associate at his firm at the age of 19. What about Brandon Fleisher, a 17-year-old investor who tripled his investments in two years—from $48,000 to $147,000?

Like many other successful people, Fleisher prioritizes sharing his knowledge, so that others can reach the same level of success.

And you can do the same. You may not have the same access to the media as these superstar players, but you can play a big role in helping others get over the mistaken belief that investment is only for people who already have wealth.

This is *your* chance to help another young person find the guidance they need.

By leaving a review of this book on Amazon, you can help a teen or young adult embark on the exciting, lucrative, engaging journey of investment and building passive wealth.

When you leave your honest opinion of this book and how it's helped you on Amazon, other readers will be able to tell whether it's the right book for them – and you can be the change their financial future needs.

Thank you for helping people like you find the guidance they're looking for. This is a team effort, and I couldn't do it without you.

6

WHAT THE RICHEST 20% DO DIFFERENTLY TO BUILD THEIR WEALTH

I t seems like one day, I just woke up, and everybody was talking about passive income. I see all these hacks on social media on how you can make a passive income, and it seems like a lot of people are doing it. However, according to the US Census Bureau, only about 20% of American households actually earn a passive income (Chamber of Commerce, 2021). So, with all of this hype, why aren't people doing it? This is a great question, and I believe that a lot of it has to do with the fact that people simply don't understand how to make a passive income or even what it is to begin with. It sounds like a great idea, but without the steps to guide you, it can just be something we think is out of reach.

The good news is that everybody can make a passive income, even if it's not in the same way. It is important to learn more about a passive income because it allows you to build your wealth without being actively involved. This doesn't mean it's free money, but it also doesn't mean that you're not going to be limited by the amount of time you are able to put in. If this still seems a bit strange to you, don't worry; we are going to cover it all in this chapter.

PASSIVE INCOME 101

Many people believe that passive income is money without working. To some extent, this can be true, but it doesn't just happen on its own. You need to put in work at some level in order to make a passive income. Many forms of passive income mean that you are going to put in a specific amount of work at the beginning, and then whatever you've worked on generates income long after you have stopped working. This means you can bring in money without actively doing something. A 9-to-5 job cannot be a passive income because you have to go to work every day in order to get paid. A musician who has worked on and released a song can make a passive income by selling and streaming the track. This money will keep coming in for the musician long after they have finished the work of writing and producing the music. Do you see the difference between the two? It's not that the musician doesn't do any work, but it's that the work has continuous value over time.

The basic idea is that you need to create something that's going to provide you with a continuous stream of money. When you have a source of passive income, you give yourself the opportunity to make a lot more money than with a normal job. The reason for this is that passive income is not limited by your skill or the time you have to give to it. When you work most jobs, you will need to give a specific amount of time in order to complete projects or do the work, and then you can get paid for the time you have put in. Even if you are young, your time is always going to be limited. We only have 24 hours in a day, and you also need to take care of your own needs. This means you can't be working the entire 24 hours. There is a limited amount of energy and mental brainpower that you can put into the tasks. Once you have used this up for the day, you will not be able to make any more money from it.

When it comes to passive income, these limitations don't necessarily exist. You will be able to rely less on your salary and lean into earning money in a passive way. This is a great way to buy your freedom from the traditional workforce. If you don't see yourself working a 9 to 5 for the rest of your life, it is also a great way to increase your income, even if you are earning minimum wage at a traditional job. It gives you more options and allows you to reach your financial goals a lot quicker.

Many people from the older generation don't really think about passive income because they rely a lot on their regular salary. This is unfortunate because it means that they can only build wealth from one stream. Passive income means that you can have more than one source of income, so if something were to happen in one area, you still have yourself covered by the others. This allows you to feel a lot more secure with your finances, and you don't have to stress out if you lose your job or want to change careers and need to take a salary cut. It is very common for people to switch careers and try something new in their life, and if you have this passive income to fall back on, you won't be scared to do it. This gives you a much bigger chance to build a life that you really want to live.

While there are plenty of ways you can make a passive income, there are a few different categories that they can fall under. The first way you can make a passive income is to buy into it or invest. Many types of investing give you a chance to make a passive income because after you have chosen your investment and put in the money, you can leave it to grow. If you invest in dividends, stocks, bonds, and real estate, you'll be making some form of passive income. When it comes to real estate, it generally depends on how you are using it. If you are just purchasing a property to sell it at a higher price later, then this can be a form of passive income. However, flipping the property and using it as a rental property won't be.

House flipping is when you purchase a property at a low price and then do the work to renovate and decorate it. Once this process is over, you can sell the house for a much higher price, and you'll make a profit from this. If you choose to do this, you need to do your research to make sure whatever property you're buying is in the right location and actually has potential buyers for it. You will also need enough money to renovate the house. A rental property is when you purchase a property and rent it out to other people. This can be a form of passive income or a form of active income. If you purchase the property and rent it out to a long-term renter, then it will be a more passive form of income. You could sign a lease with the renter for 12 months, and this means you don't really have to do anything for those 12 months, but you will be getting money each month. However, this will make you a landlord, so if there are any problems with the property, you'll have to go in and fix it. The other type of rental property that exists is more for short-term or vacation rental. You cannot think of it more like an Airbnb because renters only stay there for a few days while they are on vacation. If you own a rental property like this, you'll have to make sure that the property is clean and ready to go for the next group of people who want to stay there. As you can see, it's not always clear-cut when it comes to passive and active income.

The other type of passive income is when you create something. You'll be doing work upfront so that it can generate income over time. This is a like the example of the musician. After putting in the work to write and produce the song, the musician doesn't have to do much more work in order to make money from it. As long as people are streaming the song, then money will be coming in. Writing a book or designing a template would be similar in terms of generating passive income. One thing you have to consider when you are creating something is that there is usually a shelf life to these items. There are very few things that are truly timeless. At some point, the song or the book is not going to generate as much income as it did at the beginning. This is why most artists don't only produce one thing in their lives.

If you want to get a better idea of this, all you have to do is go onto YouTube and look up a famous YouTuber.

Scroll down to one of the earlier videos and see when the last comments came in. Creating YouTube videos is a way to make passive income because after you have created the video, you can continue collecting income for as long as people are watching it. You will notice that even if the YouTuber is a big name, the older YouTube videos do not get as many new views or as many interactions. This means they are not making as much money from the older YouTube videos as they did at the beginning. This is why they have to continue to push out content in order to make money. There might be a few videos that are truly timeless and still generating income after a long time, but that will not be the majority.

WHY PASSIVE INCOME IS THE KEY TO A WEALTHY LIFE

There are tons of reasons you should get into creating a passive income stream for yourself. The sooner you do it, the better because you can benefit from it for quite a long time in the future. It also helps you to build skills and gives you more money to work with. In this section, we are going to be going through a few of the best reasons to prioritize creating a passive income in your life.

Extra Cash Flow

This one is definitely a no-brainer. When you create a passive income, you bring in more money. Every person would love a bit extra to help with their financial goals and just to stop stressing over money. When you create a passive income, you have more control over the money coming in, and it's not just dependent on your regular 9-to-5 job. If you are still in school or college, you can create a passive income to help you pay for your study fees or just to let you have more spending money. Since you typically have more time while you are studying, you can use this wisely to find different types of passive income streams to help build your passive income portfolio. This way, it's already set up when you are ready to enter the workforce. You won't have to settle for a job that pays you too little just because you're desperate for money. This is always a huge positive when it comes to building a passive income.

Frees up Your Time

Time will always be your greatest asset, and what you use it for will determine whether you are successful. Every person has the same amount of time in the day, but what differentiates the successful and those who are not successful is what they do with it. Time is more valuable than money because you can always make more money, but the same can't be said about time. Everybody likes to focus on managing their money, but we also need to focus on managing our time. When you create a passive income for yourself, you begin to free up your time so you can do things that you really want to do.

This is such an important concept to grasp so you don't get caught up in working so hard and that you never get to enjoy your life. Working hard is essential if you want to be successful, but it doesn't mean you have to kill yourself to do it. When you have a passive income, it becomes a lot easier for you to find balance in your life.

Some people work hard so they can create a passive income stream that can cover all of their daily needs. This means they can choose a job because they love it rather than because they absolutely need the money. Many people want to work in areas they are passionate about but are not able to because of the money aspect. When you have a passive income that is enough to cover everything that you need no longer have to think about this when you are picking a career or choosing what you want to do with the rest of your life. There's so much freedom in this, and it helps you to build a life that you are proud of living.

Reduces Your Stress About the Future

It seems like everything we do is for the future and not for today. Many of our financial goals are simply about the future and making sure that we can have enough money to survive in retirement or another future date. This is not a bad thing because we definitely need to plan for the future, but the problem is that when we only think about the future, we become incredibly stressed. The future can be a very scary place because we don't know what's going to be there. This might even be more so for somebody who's in school or college and doesn't know what the future is going to look like for them. Let me let you in on a little secret; even adults don't know what the future holds. They might look like they have all the answers and great plans for the coming years of their life, but many of us are just winging it. We can all put plans together, but sometimes life doesn't work out that way. It doesn't mean we shouldn't plan, but we do have to be prepared for the uncertainty that comes with the future.

The meaning of life, uncertainties have to do with finances, so when you have a passive income, it brings security to your life. You know that you're going to have enough money to hold you over and to make it. You won't have to worry about living paycheck to paycheck or trying to do various side hustles to bring in money. You know that you're going to have enough, and this is such a great feeling. When you are less stressed about the future, you allow yourself to make better decisions. The number of bad decisions we make when we are stressed or anxious can be quite shocking. If having a passive income helps alleviate some of the stress and anxiety, then that is a good enough reason to get going.

Can Use It to Build a Nomadic Lifestyle

For those of you who have a passion for travel and seeing the world, this is a huge benefit. Passive income means that you can earn money from wherever you are in the world. This means you are earning money when you are at your home, and you can earn money in a remote cabin in the woods somewhere in the Netherlands or wherever else you want to travel. Most people I know would love to travel more and see the world, but they simply cannot leave their jobs for that amount of time, or they do not have the money to do it. A passive income completely solves this problem.

If you save enough money in your regular job, you can probably take a week or two off to go to your favorite destination, but this might not be enough for many people. Imagine living in another country for three months and really embarrassing yourself in the culture there. Maybe you can learn a new skill and get to know the locals and broaden your idea of the world. This can be an amazing experience that a passive income could help you do. You could live in different areas of the world, so you don't have to be tied down just because of your job. This lifestyle is not for everybody, but it gives you the option when you have a passive income.

Provides Financial Stability

The world is a crazy place, and any place where we can find some sort of stability, we need to grab it. People always talk about getting a regular job at a big company so they can have stability, but in most cases, this is not true stability. At the end of the day, you are putting your future in the hands of another person or company. Anything could happen, and you could lose your job, or you could take a pay cut. An example that might be close to home is what happened during the COVID-19 pandemic. Nobody expected that to hit as hard as it did, and so many people lost their jobs and sources of income. This was definitely not something that could've been planned, but it resulted in many people struggling financially. Recessions are also quite common, even though people might not realize it. This means the economy takes a hit, and it becomes a lot more difficult to make ends meet for a regular person.

All of this means that getting to a place where you are financially stable is important. It means that you can take care of yourself, even though there might be crazy things happening in the world. You are not fully reliant on any one source of income or a job to provide for you. This might not be something you are thinking about right now, but as you get older, it's going to be more and more important. This is because you're going to have people that are relying on you, and you will have more responsibilities as an adult.

Having a passive income also means that you have to be more financially educated. Since you have money coming in from a source that is not a traditional job, you will need to know how to work out your income and the taxes that come with it. A person working a regular job does not think about these things as much as somebody who is earning income on the side. It gives you a window into the financial world, and you can make plans to ensure your finances are secure. This is a huge benefit of a passive income because it gives you the opportunity to learn more about your own finances. You will be able to make plans and prepare better for things that can come in the future.

IDEAS FOR BUILDING PASSIVE INCOME STREAMS

Now that we have gone through all the benefits of a passive income, you might be really excited to get going. Before you can make a passive income, you will need an idea. You will need to know what you should be doing in order to make some extra money. The good news is that there are so many options, so you are probably going to find one that suits you. We are going to go through a list of different passive income ideas and give a short explanation of what they are. If you find one that piques your interest, why not do some additional research on it so you can figure out whether this is something you want to start? You might start something and realize that is not what you want to do, and that's perfectly okay. You have time to sift through all these ideas until you find one that works for you.

Create a Course

Online courses are becoming very popular because people want to learn new skills but also don't want to pay an arm and a leg for it. If you create a course, you can upload it on a place like Skillshare or Udemy, and if people subscribe or purchase your course, you'll get money for it. I will say that if you really want to make a good amount of money from your course, you will need to provide a decent amount of value to your customers. This means you can't make a course on something you know nothing about. You don't have to be an expert, and you don't have to have a degree, but you do need to have the knowledge to help people learn the skill they want.

There are so many different skills that you could teach online, so don't just think it's about academics. If you are good at math, then you can teach a math course online, but some people are more creative. In this case, you could teach painting or music. If you are going to college for something, you might want to teach something in line with that since you have credentials for it. Look at what you're good at in the skills you have and see if there is a demand for that knowledge; then you know you will be able to teach a good course that will provide value to your students and bring in additional money.

Write an Ebook

If you have a passion for writing, then why not write an ebook? You can sell your ebook on distribution sites, such as Amazon, which reaches millions of readers. Every time somebody purchases your book, you will get a profit from it. When you write this book, make sure you are writing on a topic you know about. This is very similar to creating a course, but it's in a different format.

You might also want to go a more creative route and write a fiction book. This is a book where you will tell a story rather than teach something more technical. Whether you are writing something to give information or to entertain, you just need to make sure there is an audience for it. Once the book is written, you just need to publish it and wait for people to purchase it.

Affiliate Marketing

Affiliate marketing is how many social media influencers make their money. If you were ever wondering how social media influencers can afford their lifestyles, well, you have found the answer. You'll notice that a lot of influencers have a link where you can click to purchase items on other sites. For example, an influencer that is all about living a healthy life would have a link in a profile where you can purchase supplements or workout clothes. Every time you click on the link and buy something, the influencer will get a cut of the profit. They are basically just marketing for the company and getting paid to do that.

Anybody who has a social media page, website, or blog will be able to use affiliate marketing. There are tons of companies that generate affiliate links, such as Amazon and eBay. When it comes to making money through affiliate links, you will need to have a good number of people following you. It is also a good idea to make sure whatever you are promoting is something that your followers would be interested in. An influencer who is all about healthy living will probably not make that much money from an affiliate link that leads to a candy store. This is because the people who are following this influencer want to see health content. The type of content you create and the type of information you put out will determine what kind of affiliate links will be most beneficial for you and your followers.

Retail Arbitrage

Arbitrage might sound like a big word, but all it means is that you are reselling an item for a higher price than what you bought it for. Many people do this on sites like Amazon and eBay. You can find an item for quite cheap on a different site and then advertise and sell it on those platforms. This is great because you don't actually have to make any items. All you're doing is reselling it at a higher price. Just make sure the price you are reselling it for is not too high. Otherwise, you will not get many buyers and won't make that big of a profit.

Amazon and eBay take most of the work out of this process. They have warehouses that will store the items as well as shop and handle it as well. They will take a portion of the profit, but it is worth it since you're not going to be doing much of the work. All you have to do is make sure that the items are available at the warehouses, and you are set.

Buy Crowdfunded Real Estate

Real estate investing is something that is attractive to many people, but getting into it can be difficult. You need a good amount of money in order to get started, and most people do not have this money, especially if you are a young adult or a teenager. Investing in real estate also means you have to do a lot of the legwork in terms of finding clients and handling them if anything were to go wrong. You also have to consider maintenance management and repairs, which are all big jobs. This is where crowdfunding comes into play. What happens is a team of investors get together and look into the real estate available on the market. They will pick one that seems profitable, and then other people can choose to invest in the property. You can choose to invest as much as you feel comfortable with investing.

Then you will get returns from the profits that you made through the real estate investment. This is very similar to investing in the stock market, but instead of investing in companies, you're investing in individual properties.

One thing to consider with this type of investment is there is no guarantee that you will actually make any money. Crowdfunding works differently from the stock market in various ways, so you cannot rely on it in the same way. Plus, there is not as long of a track record with it. You will have to make sure that you have done your research and then make a judgment call based on that. The good news is that since an experienced team of investors has chosen the property, you do have a good chance of making a good amount of passive income. With all this being said, it's definitely not a good idea to have all of your money tied up in these types of investments since real estate is quite sensitive to economic downturns, so you do have to bear this in mind.

Invest in REITs

Coming in hot with another idea for those who want to invest in real estate but don't have the capital to go all in. REIT stands for real estate investment trust. This is just referring to a company or team that chooses to invest in and manage real estate. The majority of the income that is made through property investments will be distributed to their shareholders. This means that it gives you an opportunity to invest in real estate without actually owning any property. You can invest in a REIT through the stock market since it acts like any other dividend stock. You will get paid out at regular intervals, just like a dividend which means you have the opportunity to make some passive income through this.

Start a Blog

If you are a talented writer with some information on basically any topic, you can start a blog. Everybody is looking for information on the internet, and written information is still of great value. Once you have started your blog, you can sell ad space or get sponsors, and this will generate some income. Why not go to a random blog today and see all the different ads that pop up when you use it? It's usually in the form of banner ads all along the side of the webpage. The owner of the blog is getting paid for all of this.

Sponsorships work a bit differently. In order to get sponsors, you need to have a good number of people following your work. You will also need to be in specific niches that sponsors find interesting and where they would be able to connect with more buyers. If you have a passion for hunting or fishing, a store that sells hunting and fishing equipment would be more likely to sponsor you than a skincare brand. You can reach out to sponsors, or they can reach out to you, and all you have to do is promote their products on your page in order to get paid. The terms and conditions will differ based on the company and the deal that you strike with them. Some people choose to hire managers to help them with their social media and blog income. This is completely up to you, but you don't have to do it at the beginning. Rather focus on growing your audience.

You could also cross-market yourself on various platforms. You might notice that many social media influencers have multiple social media pages running across different platforms. Someone who has a blog will also have a YouTube channel, an Instagram page, and maybe even a TikTok. This allows them to make money and promote themselves on these various platforms but use the same type of content. You can write a blog post on a certain subject and make a video on the exact same one. Then you can market it on your Instagram or TikTok and use pieces of the information to create content on these short-form content platforms. You only have to think about the content once, and you can post on all platforms. This is also a great way to make sure that you are getting more followers and views. If you happen to go viral on one platform, it will be a lot easier for you to go viral on others because of cross-promotion. Then you can use sponsors and affiliate marketing on all your platforms to bring in money from multiple streams.

Sell Designs

If you are a creative person who enjoys drawing or designing, then you can utilize these skills to sell some designs online. There are plenty of ways you can make money through doing this, including selling printed T-shirts or selling templates online. Etsy is one platform that allows you to do this, and so are CaféPress and Zazzle. The two former companies sell items such as mugs and T-shirts, but you design what goes on them. They will take care of the printing and distribution of the item, and all you have to do is make the design. Every time somebody buys a T-shirt or hat with your design on it, you will get some profit from that.

When it comes to a platform such as Etsy, you'll be able to sell templates and downloadable designs. If you have a template for a résumé or perhaps a drawing, you can upload it to Etsy, and people can purchase it from the website. Since it is in a downloadable format, you don't have to worry about shipping or packaging the item. As soon as somebody buys it, it will be sent to them, and they can use it for what they like. I have also seen some people designing coloring pages or homework pages. There are probably thousands of things you can design if you get creative with it.

HOW TO KNOW WHICH PASSIVE INCOME IDEA WORKS FOR YOU

We have just scratched the surface when it comes to passive income ideas. There are so many of these out there, and you need to know which one is going to work best for you. In this section, we are going to be talking about how you can know if a passive income idea is going to suit you. There are a few things that you need to do to figure this out, but once you have discovered the best avenue for your passive income, you can run with it.

List Out Your Top Five Skills and Interests

The first thing you will need to do is discover what you are good at or what you're interested in. This is a good place to start because you can use skills you already have to generate income. Alternatively, you can learn about something you are interested in. Starting up a passive income stream with something that interests you will have a higher likelihood of succeeding because you're motivated to keep going. If you absolutely hate cars or don't care about them, then there's no point in starting a YouTube channel all about cars. You're probably not going to put in as much effort as you should and will be bored when you are creating content. But if you love cars and know a lot about them, then you can definitely start a YouTube channel on it since you'll be motivated to find out more and create content that your subscribers will love.

Writing a list of your skills and interest will help you to see where you can start. Keep your list to just five because you don't want to overwhelm yourself with options. Once you have your list, you can then decide which of your options will be able to make you money and which one's probably won't. If you have multiple options, then you can try them all out and see how they work and see if they fit into your schedule or lifestyle.

Think About How Much Time You're Willing to Devote

Every side hustle is going to take some time and some resources from you. You need to decide how much you are willing to give to your side hustle for it to start generating income. Some passive streams of income will take more work than others. This means you will only be able to receive an income from it once it has taken off. Much of the work you have been doing up until that point is probably not going to give you that much money or sustain you in any way.

Think about how much time you truly have to give toward your form of passive income and if you need to start off with some sort of capital or money towards it. If you need money to start up your income stream, then you need to work on a plan to gain this income before you get started. All of this takes time and planning. If you are too busy to work on your first choice of passive income, then you can choose something else until your time frees up.

Consider How Much Money You Stand to Make With Each Potential Idea

You want to make sure that whatever passive form of income you are moving towards will have income potential. This means that you will be able to make money from your hustle. It's all well and good to be passionate about something or to enjoy doing it, but if it's not making any money, then it is simply a hobby. You can have as many hobbies as you would like, but you can't call all of them a passive income.

If you are trying to figure out how much money you could potentially make from your side hustles, you can do some research. Look for people who are doing something similar to what you want to do and see what they are making and the lifestyles they are living. This will help you to decide whether your income idea is actually going to be worth it. If nobody is doing anything remotely close to what you plan on doing, it might be an indication that it is not a good idea, or you could be innovative. Explore the ideas a bit more and see what is going on around you. You should never be afraid to do research and find out the pros and cons of the things you want to do. It's just going to help you make better decisions in the future.

Think About Your Timeline

I know most of us would love to start a passive income stream and just watch the money rolling in immediately, but this is usually not the case. You are going to have to wait at least a few weeks or months before your passive income stream can start working for you. This is why it is important to work on a timeline for yourself. Setting a timeline is essential for most of the goals in your life, as we have discussed in Chapter 1.

Some income streams are going to take a while to set up, and that means you will have to put off earning money for as long as it takes. On the other hand, there might be certain avenues that generate income a lot quicker. You need to decide when you need the money.

Since you are probably in your early 20s or late teen years, you have the luxury of time. You can make a plan to set up your passive income streams and work on it for a few months or years before you actually need the money. Don't be put off just because it's going to take a while to get started. Now is the time to get the ball rolling because as soon as you start working on your career or have full adult responsibilities, that's going to take up a lot of your energy and a lot of your resources. You truly will never have as much time as you have right now, so it is always a good idea to put in as much work as you possibly can.

Narrow Down Your Options by Asking Yourself These Questions

After you have done all that, you should take some time to ask yourself the following questions to help narrow down exactly what you want to do. You might have tons of options or maybe only have a few. These questions will help you dig a little deeper so you can find out the best plan or move forward.

Why Do You Want to Do This?

Simon Sinek wrote a book called *Start with Why* (Davies, n.d.). It was one of those books that went viral because the concepts in it changed the way people thought. He spoke about how when you know why you are doing things it is so much easier to be motivated and to motivate others. Companies that think about why they are doing things tend to have a far bigger following and are more successful. They also share the "why" with the people who work for them, and this brings them on board, so they're all loyal contributors and workers in the company.

This might sound like a very small thing, but knowing why you are doing something can be incredibly powerful. It is a motivating factor, so if you feel like you are running low on momentum, you can think back to why you are doing it, and you can find what you need to keep going. Your reasoning could be a myriad of different things; you just need to find out what it is. It could be that you are working toward becoming financially free or another specific financial goal. Perhaps your passive income stream is something you are passionate about, and you want to do good with that. Once you have your "why," take some time and write it down so you don't forget it.

What Can You See Yourself Doing in the Long Run?

Starting a passive income stream is like a long-term relationship and not like a one-time blind date. A one-time date, you can leave or cut it short if you are not enjoying yourself, but if you are in a long-term relationship, you stick it out even through the bad parts. If you can't see yourself doing your side hustle or passive income stream for the long term, then it probably isn't for you.

You might need to work on your ideas, but every day or each week, carve out time to put into it. If you don't do this, then your income stream might completely fail and not be as successful as you would like it to be, and perhaps it might not even get off the ground in the first place. If you absolutely hate whatever you are doing, then there's no point in even starting it because you aren't going to follow through.

How Will Doing This Impact Your Schedule?

Look at your current schedule and see if you have the time or the resources to put into a side hustle or an extra stream of income. You need to be realistic with the time that you have, as well as whether your schedule will accommodate your plans.

What Is Something That Feels More Like Play Than Work?

If you can find something that feels more like a hobby or something fun that you enjoy doing, then this is a great side hustle or passive income stream. It means that you aren't going to feel like it's work or something you are forced to do. If you love sports, then you are probably the first one on the field, and you make sure you are present for all the games and practices. If you absolutely hate sports, then you are likely trying to avoid it at all costs and look for excuses as to why you can't make it to sessions. The same can be said with basically anything else in life. If you can find something that you really enjoy, it's going to be easy for you to continue.

What Can You Offer That Few Others Can?

If you're planning to set up a business type of side hustle, then you need to start looking at what you are offering people who will be purchasing or subscribing to you. If one-million people are offering the exact same thing, what makes you different, and what makes you stand out? This doesn't mean that you have to make something brand new or reinvent the wheel. You just have to offer something slightly different that will add value to other people.

I recently started following a fitness influencer who, on the surface, looked like every other fitness influencer. He shared his workouts and showed what he ate in a day. He also gave tips and tricks on losing weight and building muscle. All of these things are pretty standard when it comes to a fitness influencer. When I started following him, he only had a few thousand followers, but over the course of just a few months, his followers skyrocketed, and his courses were selling out. I'm going to be honest; the information that he was putting out was information that you could probably find from 1,000 other influences in the same space. However, he was doing something different.

He was showing other people how to be a fitness influencer, giving them tips and tricks on the sort of cameras and equipment they need to create content like he is. He also added humor to his content that entertained people while giving them the information they needed. He was not only knowledgeable about what he was doing, but he was also entertaining. That is a rare combination and something that clearly attracted tons of people. It's not that he was doing something so different from the other people out there, but that he was delivering it in a different way. He was showing off his personality, and it really worked for him.

When you are thinking about what you can offer others, it's not about becoming somebody who invents brand-new ways of doing things. You might just need to come up with a different angle, and that will be enough. If you look at what other people are doing and you notice there is a missing component or a missing link, then you can be the person who adds this in. This can almost guarantee you a space in whatever market you choose to be in.

BUILD YOUR INVESTMENT PLAN

In this chapter, we had a look at quite a few passive income streams that you could try. If one or two of them spoke to you, write them down. What do you need to do in order to pursue that? If none of the suggestions spoke to you, do some research, and find about five ideas that you think might work for you. Follow the same pattern of writing out the pros and cons. Once you have your list, you can ask yourself the questions in the above section. This will help you get into the nitty-gritty of things and truly understand what passive income stream you should go ahead with.

7

HOW TO MAKE YOUR FIRST INVESTMENT

66 *Invest for the long haul. Don't get too greedy,*
and don't get too scared.

— SHELBY M.C. DAVIS

HOW-TO GUIDE

Having a specific how-to guide on the steps needed to make your first investment is so helpful. I truly wish I had this when I first started making investments because it would've made the process a lot easier. Even though I eventually figured it out, it does take some time and some trial and error. If you can skip all the hard parts and figure out the best way to get going, it's going to be a lot smoother for you.

Bear in mind that you probably are still going to make a few mistakes while you're getting used to investing, and this is completely normal. I just want to make sure you are set in the right direction from the start.

One thing that is important to realize is that investing is not an all-or-nothing type of thing. You can invest in multiple different areas and have various types of investments running at the same time. Investing is very personalized, so don't think that you have to go all in to get something out. Feel free to invest whatever amount you are comfortable with and then work to build up from there.

Look at What's Already Working/Making Money

There are already people who have gone before us, and they have invested in certain items that are working for them. It could be a good idea to look at what is already working for people and making them money. This way, you can have a higher chance of investing in something that will bring in a profit for you. This is not a sure-fire way to increase your investment capital, but it definitely can give you a good starting point. Make sure you are doing your research regardless of how you choose to make your investments because even if the crowd is doing something, it doesn't always mean that it is right.

Consider How Much Money You Want to Invest

It is definitely a good idea to take some time to consider how much money you have to invest. The best strategy for investing is to do it on a consistent basis so it becomes a habit. This means you should budget for your investments. If you're investing in a fund or in the stock market, you can budget a specific amount each month. If you are looking to invest in something that requires a larger amount for you to get started, then you can put a portion of the money needed into a savings account each month. Once you have saved up enough, then you can go ahead and make a larger investment. This way, you are still building up the habit, and you're making it more reasonable for yourself. The amount of money you are looking to invest will also help you decide what investments you should be making.

First, Have an Emergency Fund

Before you even think about investing, you need to have an emergency fund. In one of the previous chapters, we mentioned emergency funds and why they are so important. You need to have an emergency fund just in case you run into a bump in the road. If you have your emergency fund, then you will still be able to continue with your investment plan, and an emergency won't completely derail you. You will also be able to leave your money in your investments instead of needing to take it out to cover the emergency. This is essential when it comes to investing because you don't want to remove your investment unnecessarily.

Think About How Much Money You Want to Make and By When

We all have financial and money goals. Maybe one of yours is that you want to make a certain amount of money by a certain time. Knowing how much time you have before you want to have a certain amount of money is a great starting point because it means you can create a plan for how you are going to reach that goal. You will think about what you need to do and how much you need to invest. If it is not reasonable, then you can extend the time and change up your goals a little bit. Knowing this piece of information can also help you decide which investment will be best for you.

If You're Investing in Financial Products, Find a Platform

Financial products are things like mutual and index funds. A financial service provider is where you will need to go to invest. You will work with a broker that will sign you up with the platform and help you make your investments. Choosing the right platform is essential. Make sure you do your research and pick one that offers you the greatest benefits and where the fees are not as large. If you are still a student, you might be able to take advantage of student discounts and benefits, so make sure you ask about this.

Balance Your Long-Term and Short-Term Investments

Depending on the timeframe in which you want your investments to mature, you will need to choose different investment vehicles. For a short-term investment, you might need to choose something like a high-yield savings account or a certificate of deposit because you will have access to this money quicker. For long-term investments, you can investigate mutual and index funds since you can leave your money to grow for a longer period of time. With these kinds of financial products, the longer you leave them to grow, the better it's going to be for you.

This is why it is so important to understand what your financial goals are and know what you're putting your money away in. You will not be able to have one account for all your financial goals because the timelines and what you need are going to be completely different. If you have a short-term goal and put all your money into the stock market, the is a risk that the market will have a turndown. This means you will have less money than you need, and it could cause a big problem. The stock market is all about long-term gains, which is why people prefer to put money in the stock market for long-term goals.

Monitor Your Portfolio

One huge mistake I see people making all the time is that they invest in a fund or into their portfolio and leave it for a few years later without checking it. A lot of investments do run on their own, and you might not need to take any action, but it's so important for you to monitor what is going on. Check-in with your investment every month or every few months to make sure that everything is going according to plan. You might need to make some changes, so it is a good idea to know what's happening.

Keep Learning

Investing is all about continuous learning. It is important for you to understand that there are some things you just won't know about right now. There might also be some new investments that pop up in the next 10 years. If you are willing to continue to learn, you'll put yourself in a good position for your investments.

You can sign up for newsletters or blogs that talk about investing. Make sure you are following investors and finance gurus on social media so you're always getting new information about what is going on in the financial world. This doesn't mean that you always have to listen to what these people say, but if you are always thinking about your investments and your finances, you can stay on top of things.

THE STORY OF BRANDON FLEISHER

I speak to a lot of teenagers and young adults who feel they don't have to think about investing until they are much older. This might be because they don't think it's necessary to start now or because they don't think it's going to make that much of a difference to the future. I hope this story will change your mind if you are also sitting in this camp.

Brandon Fleisher (Gillespie, 2015) started out his investing journey when he was just 13 years old. He didn't invest any money, but there was an assignment in his math class where he had to pick a stock and follow along to see how it grew or plummeted. From here, it sparked something in him to learn more about investing for himself. He started investing in smaller stocks that weren't as well known. This was different from many new investors' strategies, but it worked for him.

He made sure to do as much research as he possibly could before he made his decisions. He found one company that he really believed in, and he invested. Eventually, he found that he had a real knack for investing, and he was picking the right stocks that seemed to grow quite quickly. Remember, this was not dumb luck. Brandon did the work and the research to make sure that he was choosing the right stocks.

He also made it a priority to get in contact with as many investors as he could. This way, he was able to get information from people who were much more experienced and older than him. He could ask one-on-one questions and get advice as he continued to invest. There is something to be said about the experience of people who have been in the investing game for much longer than us.

One year he invested $48,000 and managed to triple the investment in just two years. By the time he was 17 years old, he was sitting with $147,000 in investment capital. That is more than most adults can say and more than many teenagers his age had. Instead of doing things that normal teenagers did, he spent a lot of his time researching and learning. This helped him to grow in his investment journey and helped him to make the best choices he possibly could.

At this point in his life, he shares his knowledge with people around him through social media, blogs, and articles. He is still on his investment journey and continues to talk to investors who are quite prominent in the field. This way, he continues to learn and grow. He also founded the company called the Financial Bulls, which shares information about investors and the market for free.

If you thought that you could never achieve something great at a young age, you can just look at the story and understand that anything is possible. You are never too young to get started with investing, and you can make a difference in your financial future starting now. You just need to take the initiative and get going. You will look back on this time and be so thankful that you made some sacrifices and learned the skills you needed. This is what's going to set you up for your future and ensure that you are always going to be financially secure.

BUILD YOUR INVESTMENT PLAN

It is time to put some action to what you have learned. Start by creating a mini plan for yourself that will outline the actions that you need to take to make your first investment. Make sure this is a step-by-step plan so you can check off each step as you go through the process. Most of what you need is going to be in this chapter, so it won't be that much work. Creating this plan solidifies it in your mind and ensures that you are going to do something about it. You can also have a look at what you have done in the previous chapters to help you create this plan.

Once you have your investment plan, you will need to know how to manage your portfolio. This is essential to any investor, and it's why we have an entire chapter dedicated to it. You will learn a few tips and tricks that will help you along your investment journey and ensure that your investment portfolio is always going to be working for you. That is what we will be covering in the next chapter.

8

MONEY-MAKING TIME— MANAGING YOUR PORTFOLIO

> *Waiting helps you as an investor, and a lot of people just can't stand to wait. If you didn't get the deferred-gratification gene, you've got to work very hard to overcome that.*
>
> — CHARLIE MUNGER

TIPS FOR PROFITABLE PORTFOLIO MANAGEMENT

So, you've got your investment portfolio, and now what? The journey doesn't stop there. You are going to need to manage your portfolio to make sure that it's going to continue working in your favor. There are a few tips and tricks that you can use to help you manage your portfolio better. We are going to be talking more about this in this section.

Think Long-Term

It is all good to have short-term goals, but most types of investing should be done with the long term in mind. Long-term investing is what's going to make you the most amount of money over time. Remember, investing is not a get-rich-quick scheme.

Don't Try to Play the Market

Every so often, there is a finance guru that comes out, saying they have the best-kept secret for investing. This usually means they are trying to play the market to get other people to buy into their strategy. Most of these strategies fail within a few years, so never trust things that sound too good to be true. Playing the market is when you try and buy and sell stocks so quickly for short-term gains. There are some people that can do this successfully, but many of us are going to fail horribly. Rather stick to tried and true methods and strategies if you want to build a wall for your future.

Don't Take on More Risk Than You're Comfortable With

Investing is not just about money. You also have to take into consideration your emotional health and needs. Some people are built to take on more risk than other people, and that's perfectly normal. You must know what you're comfortable with so you can make decisions based on that. If you try and take on more risk than what you're comfortable with, you end up stressing yourself out. I know people who do this, and they are constantly checking on their investments. Every time something doesn't go to plan, it feels like the world is caving in. This is not a position you want to be in, and it is so easily avoidable.

If you're not sure about the risk that you can take, start slow and move up. If you ever feel uncomfortable with your investment, you have the power to change it into something you are more comfortable with. Just because you chose a certain strategy at some point in your life doesn't mean you can't make some changes as you invest. Your peace of mind is also important.

Keep Cash on Hand for a Rainy Day

It can be very tempting to throw all your money into investments because you want to make the most out of it, but you will need some cash for everyday spending as well as emergencies and unforeseen circumstances. Life is not able to be planned down to the minute, so make sure that you have some room for spending.

It is also important to enjoy your life now. If you save all of your money for the future and don't enjoy buying things for yourself now, your life will probably be pretty bland. You need to find a balance between now and the future. Life is meant to be enjoyed, so budget for that as well. This will make investing a lot more sustainable. If you throw all your money into investing and never have enough to do fun things or things that are important to you, you might end up resenting investing and giving it up completely. When things are too hard and just not enjoyable, it becomes very difficult to convince ourselves to keep going.

Remember to Diversify

One investment is not enough to make up your entire investment portfolio. Remember to diversify whenever you can so you have various types of investments as well as investments in different sectors. If you invest in stocks and bonds, make sure your stocks are diversified as well. You can always start off by investing in one or two things, but as your investment portfolio grows, you should expand it to different areas. This will help to protect you from losing money if the market does turn sideways. It just provides you with an added layer of security.

Rebalance Your Portfolio When Needed

Rebalancing your portfolio means that you are looking at your investment and making changes to ensure that your risk is not too high. Sometimes an investment that wasn't risky when you first invested can turn into a risk later down the road. You might need to counteract this by investing in something less risky or pulling out some of the money from that investment.

As you get older, you will also need to change your investment strategies and lower your risk levels. As you get closer to your financial goals, you want to play it safer because you don't want to end up losing the money that you invested. This is a very important concept to think about so that you can reach all of your financial goals and not put stress on yourself.

BUILD YOUR INVESTMENT PLAN

If you already have an investment portfolio, why not take a look at it and see if you need to rearrange a few things? If you don't have an investment portfolio, go back to the previous chapters where you create your investment plan and see whether you have made good choices. You might notice that a few of your investments are too risky for your taste, and you might need to change your plan. Learning how to do this is essential to being successful as an investor.

Along with learning all these tips and tricks about investing and how to make the most out of it, you also need to be aware of a few traps that seem to tangle up investors. Investors often make mistakes as they move through the journey, and you will probably make one or two as well. That is why it is a good idea to know what these potential pitfalls are so you can avoid them if possible. This will put you far ahead of your peers when it comes to investing and making money.

9

THE 10 BIGGEST INVESTMENT TRAPS THAT PEOPLE FALL FOR

Did you know that Americans who had stock investments in 2022 lost over $9 trillion (Frank, 2022)? That's just the amount they lost in the stock market. Before you freak out and refuse to invest your money ever again, these losses can be avoided. Losing out on your investment is a definite possibility, and that is why we always talk about the risk involved. With this being said, investing your money is the best way to save and grow your money. If you know what some of the biggest mistakes out there are, then you can do your best to avoid them, and hopefully, you won't be part of this group that lost the $9 trillion.

THE 10 BIGGEST MISTAKES FIRST-TIME INVESTORS MAKE

There are probably hundreds of mistakes that people make when it comes to the stock market, but we are going to talk about the top 10. These are the biggest and the most common mistakes people make. If you avoid them, you will be much safer and get a lot more out of your investments.

Waiting Too Long to Start Investing

The first big mistake that people make is they wait for too long to start investing. Investing is a young person's game because they have more time. This doesn't mean that you can't start investing as an older person, but it is going to be a lot harder. When you invest as somebody in their early 20s or late teens, you have 50 or more years until retirement. This means you have a whole lot of time for your investments to grow. You can put in a small amount of money at the beginning that will suddenly pick up speed and go to something huge later on. You just need to give it time. If you are thinking about waiting until you're older to invest, please talk yourself out of that mindset because starting now is going to be crucial.

Speculating and Not Investing

This just means that you spend so much time thinking about what you're going to be investing in and mulling over the pros and cons that you never actually start investing. It can be quite scary, but it is so important to get started. Planning and preparing are necessary, but you also need to have a start date for your investing. I would suggest that you give yourself a set amount of time to do your research and plan. Once this time is up, you will have to make your first investment. Doing this means that you still give yourself time to think things over, but you don't just stop there. Once you take your first step into investing, you will be able to build momentum.

Remember, you are still young, so even if you make a bad choice, it is not the end of the world. You will probably be able to make that money back quite easily through other investments or through your income. You will also not be investing thousands of dollars right now at this point. You can make slightly riskier moves and invest in companies that are not as well known. These are stocks that could make you a lot of money in the future because their growth potential will be higher if they start small.

Not Checking Their Portfolio Regularly

Even the most passive forms of investing need to be checked on a regular basis. This is a great habit to get into when you first start investing, so you don't fall into the trap of just leaving your investments to do their own thing. Even if you have a portfolio manager, it is still important for you to know what is going on with your investments. This way, you can quickly make changes if there is an issue, and you can have peace of mind about what is going on with your investment portfolio.

Not Being Patient Enough

Investing is something that will test your patience. You will be putting your money into something that you cannot touch for at least a few years. This means that even though you're putting your money away, you can't see the benefit for a long time. We all want to be able to use our money to buy things now. This is called instant gratification and it's something many people of this generation really struggle with. If you think about it, everything we have these days happens in the blink of an eye. We have all the entertainment we could ever need on our phones. If we are hungry, we quickly order something on Postmates or Uber Eats. If we want new clothes, we can do some online shopping. Everything happened so quickly, and that has made it difficult for investors to practice patience.

You need to become comfortable with the idea of things taking years before you can use them for your benefit. Most types of investments that promise high returns in a short amount of time are typically scams. You don't want to be caught in a scam or put your money in something just because you are impatient. Investing teaches us a very important lesson about patience and realizing that the best things always come when you wait.

Not Doing Enough Research

I once knew a guy who used to play Eenie Meenie Miny Moe when he invested. He said that it was far too stressful to do research, and he knew he needed to invest money anyway. I don't think I need to tell you that the strategy did not work out. Because he didn't really understand much of what was going on in the stock market, he made a few bad decisions and lost quite a bit of money on his investments. Eventually, he realized that his plan was quite silly, and he decided to be a bit more serious. Now, he does his research before he starts investing.

The strategy of just guessing and not doing your research might seem like the easiest way to go about it right now, but it is not something you should try. You need to be able to plan and not just follow the crowd when it comes to investing. Pick stocks and investments in areas you know something about. You'll find these are the investments that perform the best. Make sure you are also doing some research while your investments are still growing because things could change, and you might need to change your strategies.

Making Decisions Based on Emotion Rather Than Logic

Emotions can truly ruin a good investment. When we use emotions as the deciding factor of our investments, we can get into a whole lot of trouble. Emotions are not reliable. You might want to invest in a company because you have some sort of emotional attachment to it. Perhaps you personally know the person who started up the company, or maybe it was the place you did your first internship. Just because you have this emotional tie doesn't mean it's going to be a good choice for your investment portfolio.

We can often overlook red flags just because there are emotions involved. Just ask anybody who has been in a bad dating relationship. Most people will be able to say there were definitely red flags. They either ignored it or they didn't see it because they loved the person. Don't get into a bad relationship with an investment. Remain levelheaded and try to remove emotions from your decisions.

Copying Other Investors' Portfolios

Many successful investors have their stock portfolios on the Internet. It takes a quick Google search to find them, and many people use those portfolios to create their own. This might sound like a great way to cheat the system because you have the formula from somebody who is already successful. Let me tell you that this is one of the biggest mistakes you can make.

This type of investing is simply lazy because you skip over doing your own research and understanding investing for yourself. While you might be able to choose the same stocks, you do not have the guarantee that it will work out the same way for you. First off, you do not know when they started investing and what their entry point was. It could be a lot more for you to invest in that same stock now, and the returns might not be as good. You also don't really know what the investor's goals are, so if they are different from yours, you will not get the results you want. Then on top of that, there might be some hidden secrets that the investor has not made public that are crucial to their investing strategy. All of these things mean that you're essentially setting yourself up for a flop. There are no quick fixes or shortcuts when it comes to investing.

Chasing Returns Instead of Focusing on Overall Financial Goals

It can be so tempting to look at an investment that is performing well right now and chase after it. The problem is that you don't know how long this upward trend is going to last, and you might get caught right in the moment when the stock starts to drop. You need to know a lot about the company before you start investing in it. Research whether there are some growth objectives and what the plans are to continue to expand a business. You will also need to do some research on the people who are high up in the company, such as the management and CEOs. Check out things like the business model to make sure that the company is setting itself up right for growth. This way, you can make a good choice for your investment rather than just looking at a short-term increase in price.

Focusing on Factors Beyond Your Control

There are going to be so many factors beyond your control when it comes to investing. These things are not your problem, and you shouldn't only be focusing on them. You can't really control things like the economy and various other factors. You can plan for issues down the road, but if something does happen that is not in your power to change, it's better not to stress yourself out about it.

Trying to Time the Market

The timing of a market strategy means that you are trying to purchase a stock at the lowest price possible and then sell it at the highest price possible in a short time frame. This is a trader mindset and not an investor mindset. The main goal here is to make as many short-term gains as possible, but it usually turns out badly for most people. The market cannot be timed. Even when you do all your research, there are things that happen in the stock market that just can't be predicted. You will end up driving yourself crazy if you try and predict every move a stock will make. This is why it is better to have a long-term investment strategy.

BUILD YOUR INVESTMENT PLAN

You know yourself better than any person out there. You might have even been thinking of making one of the mistakes that have just been listed. Being self-aware is very important when you are an investor. Think about which one of the mistakes you are most likely to make, and then write out a plan on how you can avoid it. This plan doesn't have to be pages long. Just write out a few sentences on how you can make sure you don't fall into that specific trap.

You might've been completely shocked when you read the statistics at the beginning of the chapter. While many of those Americans lost out on some form of investing, more than 64% of Americans are very likely to go broke (Dennison, 2019). At least those who are investing have tried to do something to increase their wealth, and that is more than we can say for a majority of people out there. Let's talk more about it in the next chapter.

10

PLANNING AHEAD—WHY 64% OF AMERICANS ARE HEADED FOR BROKEVILLE

T wo-thirds of Americans cannot afford to retire. This means people must work until they die and cannot afford to live a life of rest and relaxation. Not only that, but they're also going to be struggling to make ends meet at this age. This might be a scary thing to think about it, but it is a reality for many people. You don't want to put yourself in that position when you are elderly. Planning now can help prevent it.

YOUR RETIREMENT

Retirement is a long way away for you, but that doesn't mean you shouldn't plan for it. The sooner you start planning for retirement, the more money you will have at that point in your life. People are living a lot longer these days, and that means you will likely live well into retirement years. If this is the case, you want to have enough money to sustain you at that point in your life so you can enjoy your retirement the way you want to and you can make sure all your basic needs are met.

There are plenty of things that you should be considering when you start planning out your retirement. You will need to think about when you want to retire, the type of house or even country you want to live in, and your general living expenses. While you are still young, you don't have to have all the answers to these things. You might not know what your general living expenses are right now, so you're probably not going to have a good idea of what these are when you retire. Instead of getting too technical with everything, figure out how long you have until you retire and speak to older adults about their retirement plans and how much they plan to have. This will give you a better idea.

One of the best things you can do is take out a retirement investment fund that will help you to save for retirement. Many of these funds allow you to save money and get a very good return on your investment. You don't even have to invest a whole lot to get started. An IRA or a Roth IRA are good options. If you work for a company that offers a 401(k), then you should take advantage of that. You might not have the option right now, but it is always a good benefit and something to look at when you are doing interviews for positions at companies.

THE IMPORTANCE OF PLANNING FOR RETIREMENT (EVEN IF YOU DON'T HAVE A JOB YET)

It is important that you plan for your time even if you don't have a job yet. You can still plan and prepare even if you can't deposit a large amount of money into a retirement account. When it comes time for you to start investing a lot more, you'll already be used to thinking about your retirement. You will probably have a very good plan to move forward with.

Compound Interest Works in Your Favor

We have said this many times before because it is so important. Now that you are so young, you can take advantage of compound interest, and it will start to work in your favor. Turning a small amount of money into something much bigger needs a good amount of time to work for you. Simply investing a little bit of money now can see huge benefits in the future.

Keep Up With the Rising Cost of Living

The unfortunate truth is that the cost of living keeps getting higher and higher. This means that the price of items now is probably going to double or even triple by the time you get to retirement age. A lot of people believe that they can just rely on the government to pay for them in retirement, but it is not going to be enough. You want to be able to afford a good retirement rather than just struggling to make ends meet or relying on other people to help you.

Avoid Letting Inflation Eat up Your Savings

If you just put your money away in a regular savings account, you'll end up with a lot less money than you saved. Inflation means that the price of items will increase, but that doesn't mean the amount in your savings account increases with it. You will be able to afford a lot less, and all the hard work you put into saving is not going to mean much. Investing allows your money to grow faster than inflation, and this is why investing is so important.

Helps You Build up the Right Habits Instead of Breaking Bad Ones Later

A lot of investing is simply building the right habits so that you can benefit from them later. Even if you start investing a small amount of money, the main goal is to build up good habits. When you start earning more money, it's going to be like second nature, and you won't even have to think about it. Investing for your retirement is going to be your number one priority, and you will not overspend on things that are not as important. Many people who start investing at an older age really struggle because they are used to spending all their money. They have to start by investing a small percentage of their income before building it up to something that is substantial. You won't have to worry about that if you start investing a lot earlier.

You Can End up Paying More in Taxes if You Don't Start Early

Many retirement accounts are tax advantaged. This means there are significant tax benefits when you invest in them. For example, a Roth IRA allows you to pay taxes now so that you don't have to pay taxes on the money you withdraw in retirement. This means you only have to pay the current tax rate and don't have to worry about the tax percentage increasing later on. You can save a lot of money on taxes this way.

Avoid Financial Stress

Probably one of the biggest reasons you should be investing for your retirement is the simple fact that you are removing stress from your life. When you are older and getting closer to retirement, it can be incredibly stressful to save for retirement. There are so many different things you have to think about and people you might have to take care of, so it becomes incredibly stressful. If you already have your plans, you don't have to worry about all the stress, and you know that you're going to be all right.

BUILD YOUR INVESTMENT PLAN

Take some time to really think about what you want your retirement to look like. Do you want to travel the world or maybe buy a luxury car? Perhaps you would like to pick up a few new hobbies or start a small business. There are tons of opportunities when it comes to retirement because you have a lot more time. The downside is that you don't have a lot of opportunities to make more money since many jobs won't be hiring anyone at your age. If you have planned properly, then you will have the money to do whatever you want. It is important to understand the type of retirement you want so you have something to work toward, and you can start thinking about how much you will need at that point in your life.

GIVE OTHERS THE INSPIRATION THEY NEED TO MAKE THEIR FIRST INVESTMENT AND START BUILDING PASSIVE WEALTH TODAY

You now know all the ins and outs of investing for the first time. You have built your investment plan, you know how to manage your portfolio, and you are aware of the typical pitfalls to avoid.

Head over to Amazon and let other readers know how this book has helped you. Just one or two sentences could be enough to let other young people know that wealth is something they can start tasting sooner than they think.

WANT TO HELP OTHERS?

Thank you for helping me on my quest to enlighten teens and young adults on financial freedom. I hope you can help others discover how to make enough money, so they can enjoy life, see the world, and pursue their authentic passions.

CONCLUSION

Investing is such an important concept for every young person to learn. If you speak to any adult, you will quickly understand that they wish they had started investing at a younger age. If most of the population is saying the same thing, then maybe it is time for you to start taking action and investing. I don't think I have ever heard anyone say they wish they invested later in life. It's truly not about the amount of money you're investing but about building up the habit so that when you do, you have a lot of money to invest, and you have already built-up momentum. It is one of those things that you look back on in your life, and you are so thankful you did it.

Take some time to go through the investment plan that you have built. Now that you have completed the book, you have all the information you need to tweak the plan. You probably have written down or made notes of certain aspects that you might want to change. Make the changes needed so you can have an optimal investment plan.

Once you have done that, it's time to set a deadline. Your deadline is going to tell you exactly when you plan on starting to invest. The reason this is so important is so that you don't procrastinate and leave it for years and years. It can be so easy not to think about investing and one day, you'll wake up at 40 years old, and you have not planned for retirement or your future.

You are now fully equipped with everything you need to start your investing journey. The basics are the most important part because that is where most people get stuck. What you need to do is continue ironing out your plan and adjusting as you continue learning how to invest and understanding what's going to work best for you. Remember that setting clear-cut goals is always going to be the first step in anything you do. This is definitely true for your investment strategy. If you know your goals, you'll be able to motivate yourself to continue investing and getting better at doing it. You are building a skill set that is so valuable to your future and your happiness.

If you have enjoyed this book and found value in it, please take some time to give it a review on Amazon. This will help many other people who are your age and who are confused about investing to find it and get the help they need. We can create a generation of people who are ready to invest and plan for the future. You have already taken the first step on this journey, and I know you are going to make a success of yourself. I wish you nothing but luck in your investing endeavors and everything you do in your life.

REFERENCES

1FBUSA. (n.d.). *10 financial goals from real college students.* 1FBUSA. https://students.1fbusa.com/money-smarts/financial-goals-from-real-college-students

Anthony, J. (2023, January 6). *The 9 most popular stock market investing myths debunked.* StockMarketEye. https://www.stockmarketeye.com/blog/stock-investing-myths-debunked/

Bakke, D. (2022, July 26). *The top 17 investing quotes of all time.* Investopedia. https://www.investopedia.com/financial-edge/0511/the-top-17-investing-quotes-of-all-time.aspx

Barrett, C. (2021, July 15). Meet the teen investors of the future. *The Financial Times.* https://www.ft.com/content/41d016e5-9b46-4b80-8d40-4a0abbf7f6d6

Be The Budget. (2020, December 3). *10 reasons why passive income is so important.* Be the Budget. https://bethebudget.com/why-passive-income-is-important/

Bennett, R. (2022, March 8). *8 steps to choose a new bank.* Bankrate. https://www.bankrate.com/banking/how-to-choose-a-bank/

Brainy Quote. *Henry Ford Quotes.* https://www.brainyquote.com/quotes/henry_ford_384400

Brock, C. (2023, March 14). *What is passive income?* The Motley Fool. https://www.fool.com/investing/how-to-invest/passive-income/

Cabello, M. (2023, January 2). *New year, new savings plan: 5 smart tips for beginning investors.* CNET. https://www.cnet.com/personal-finance/investing/new-year-new-savings-plan-5-smart-tips-for-beginning-investors/

Carlos, A. (2022, April 28). *6 reasons why you should start retirement planning early.* District Capital Management. https://districtcapitalmanagement.com/start-retirement-planning-early/

Carlson, B. (2022, February 6). *8 of the biggest investing myths.* A Wealth of Common Sense. https://awealthofcommonsense.com/2022/02/the-8-biggest-investing-myths/

CFP, M. F. (2022, November 28). *Retirement planning: An introduction.* The Motley Fool. https://www.fool.com/retirement/

Chamber of Commerce. (2021, December 31). *Cities whose residents make the most passive income.* Chamber of Commerce. https://www.chamberofcommerce.org/cities-whose-residents-make-the-most-passive-income/

Chan, C. (2021, April 5). *Learn how to set SMART financial goals.* Credit Counselling Society. https://nomoredebts.org/blog/budgeting-saving/what-does-it-mean-to-set-smart-financial-goals

Corporate Finance Institute. (2023, March 21). *How do banks make money?* Corporate Finance Institute. https://corporatefinanceinstitute.com/resources/economics/how-do-banks-make-money/#:

Costa, M. (2023, January 29). *Average net worth by age: Where do you stand?* Clever Girl Finance. https://www.clevergirlfinance.com/blog/average-net-worth-by-age-where-do-you-stand/

Cussen, M. P. (2022, January 23). *How will your investment make money?* Investopedia. https://www.investopedia.com/articles/financial-theory/09/how-investments-make-money-income.asp#:

Daly, L. (2022, November 19). *This is the number-one investing mistake young adults make.* Www.fool.com. https://www.fool.com/the-ascent/buying-stocks/articles/this-is-the-number-one-investing-mistake-young-adults-make/

Davey, L. (2022, October 6). *What is passive income? Ultimate guide with examples.* Shopify. https://www.shopify.com/ca/blog/passive-income

Davies, S. D. (n.d.). *Book summary: Start with why by Simon Sinek.* Sam Thomas Davies. https://www.samuelthomasdavies.com/book-summaries/business/start-with-why/

Davis ETFs. (n.d.). *Wisdom of great investors – quotes.* Davis ETFs. https://www.davisetfs.com/investor_education/quotes

Dennison, S. (2019, September 23). *64% of americans aren't prepared for retirement — and 48% don't care.* Yahoo Finance. https://ca.finance.

yahoo.com/news/survey-finds-42-americans-retire-100701878.
html#:

EDUCBA. (2021, February 22). *Investment strategies | importance of investment strategies*. EDUCBA. https://www.educba.com/invest ment-strategies/

Fok, I. (2021). *Top 3 factors that determine which investment strategy is...* PyInvesting. https://pyinvesting.com/blog/14/top-3-factors-that-determine-which-investment-strategy-is-right-for-you/

Fonville, M. (2020, February 2). *9 reasons why retirement planning is important*. Covenant. https://www.covenantwealthadvisors.com/post/9-reasons-why-retirement-planning-is-important

Frank, R. (2022, September 27). *Stock market losses wipe out $9 trillion from americans' wealth*. CNBC. https://www.cnbc.com/2022/09/27/stock-market-losses-wipe-out-9-trillion-from-americans-wealth-.html

Frankel, M. (2023, February 24). *How to start investing money for the first time*. The Motley Fool. https://www.fool.com/investing/how-to-invest/

Geier, B. (2021, February 10). *10 types of investments (and how they work)*. SmartAsset. https://smartasset.com/investing/types-of-investment

Gillespie, P. (2015, April 28). *Meet the 17-year-old investor who tripled his money*. CNNMoney. https://money.cnn.com/2015/04/28/invest ing/millennial-investor-17-year-old-brandon-fleisher/

Gobat, J. (n.d.). *Banks: At the heart of the matter*. IMF. https://www.imf. org/en/Publications/fandd/issues/Series/Back-to-Basics/Banks#:

Gobat, J. (2012, March). *Finance and development*. Finance and Development | F&D. https://www.imf.org/external/pubs/ft/fandd/2012/03/basics.htm#:

Gravier, E. (2021, June 22). *Here are the 7 biggest investing mistakes you want to avoid, according to financial experts*. CNBC. https://www.cnbc.com/select/biggest-investing-mistakes/

Groww. (n.d.). *5 common stock investing mistakes to avoid as a beginner*. Groww. https://groww.in/blog/common-stock-investing-mistakes-to-avoid-as-a-beginner

Hayes, A. (2023, March 16). *Investment basics explained with types to invest*

in. Investopedia. https://www.investopedia.com/terms/i/invest
ment.asp#toc-how-an-investment-works

Henricks, M. (2022, August 4). *21 investment terms you need to know.*
SmartAsset. https://smartasset.com/investing/investment-terms-
you-need-to-know

Huddleston, C. (2019, March 14). *62% of americans don't know banking
basics -- and it's costing them.* Yahoo News. https://ca.news.yahoo.
com/62-americans-dont-know-banking-100600295.html?
guccounter=1

II, K. L. M. (2022, February 4). *5 investing myths that could cost you.*
Business   Insider.   https://www.businessinsider.com/personal-
finance/investing-myths

Johnston, M. (2021, May 30). *Why banks don't need your money to make
loans.* Investopedia. https://www.investopedia.com/articles/invest
ing/022416/why-banks-dont-need-your-money-make-loans.asp

Karr, A. (2022, September 26). *What is risk tolerance? A guide for parents
& teens.* Mydoh. https://www.mydoh.ca/learn/money-101/invest
ing/what-is-risk-tolerance-a-guide-for-parents-teens/#what-is-
risk-tolerance

Kotak Life. (2022, July 22). *How to manage your portfolio like a professional?* Kotak Life. https://www.kotaklife.com/insurance-guide/
wealth-creation/how-to-manage-portfolio-like-professional

Lake, R. (2020, October 16). *How do banks work?* Forbes Advisor.
https://www.forbes.com/advisor/banking/how-do-banks-work/

Larm, T. (n.d.). *How to start an investment portfolio.* Edward Jones.
https://www.edwardjones.com/us-en/market-news-insights/
personal-finance/investing-strategies/how-start-investment-
portfolio

Larsen, K. (2017, December 12). *How to find the right side hustle for you.*
Believe in a Budget. https://believeinabudget.com/find-the-right-
side-hustle/

Lawler, J. (2022, January 17). *How to pick an investment (that works for
you).* Www.flowbank.com. https://www.flowbank.com/en/learn
ing-center/learning-center/how-to-pick-an-investment-that-
works-for-you

Leeds, P. (2022, November 3). *10 common stock investing mistakes to avoid*. The Balance. https://www.thebalancemoney.com/common-investing-mistakes-you-must-avoid-4104189

ManuLife. (n.d.). *3 reasons why you need to plan for your retirement early*. ManuLife. https://www.manulife.com.sg/en/insights/3-reasons-why-you-need-to-plan-for-your-retirement-early.html

Mydoh. (2022, September 19). *Basic investing terms and definitions for kids & teens*. Mydoh. https://www.mydoh.ca/learn/money-101/investing/basic-investing-terms-and-definitions/

Novel Investor. (n.d.). *Quotes on diversification*. Novel Investor. https://novelinvestor.com/quote-category/diversification/#:

O'Shea, A. (2021, August 18). *Types of investments*. NerdWallet. https://www.nerdwallet.com/article/investing/types-of-investments

Panel, E. (2022, January 25). *Council post: Looking to start A side hustle? Ask yourself these 10 questions first*. Forbes. https://www.forbes.com/sites/theyec/2022/01/25/looking-to-start-a-side-hustle-ask-yourself-these-10-questions-first/?sh=2fd510304edd

Pinsent, W. (2022, June 2). *5 common mistakes young investors make*. Investopedia. https://www.investopedia.com/articles/younginvestors/09/common-mistakes-young-investors.asp

Qureshi, A. (2021, August 3). *Financial freedom*. Youth Table Talk. https://www.youthtabletalk.com/financial-freedom-and-6-reasons-why-it-is-important-for-young-students-2/

Ramsey Solutions. (2022, December 9). *4 most common types of bank accounts*. Ramsey Solutions. https://www.ramseysolutions.com/banking/types-of-bank-accounts

Reinicke, C. (2021, September 2). *Here's why it's smart to start saving for retirement when you're in your 20s*. CNBC. https://www.cnbc.com/2021/09/02/why-you-should-start-saving-for-retirement-in-your-20s.html

Royal, J. (2022, December 29). *How to start investing*. Bankrate. https://www.bankrate.com/investing/how-to-start-investing/

Royal, J. (2023, March 7). *23 passive income ideas to help you make money in 2023*. Bankrate. https://www.bankrate.com/investing/passive-income-ideas/

Schroeder, J. (2017, April 20). *The simple answer to how to invest? There isn't one*. Advance Capital Management. https://blog.acadviser.com/the-simple-answer-to-how-to-invest-there-isnt-one

Shopify. (2022, November 4). *30 best passive income ideas to build your wealth (2023)*. Shopify. https://www.shopify.com/ca/blog/passive-income-ideas#29

Stefanka, L. (2022, September 2). *Digital bank vs. traditional bank: What's best for business?* Relay. https://relayfi.com/blog/digital-bank-vs-traditional-bank

Stein, R. (2013, June 12). *Portfolio management - 10 tips for better results*. Seeking Alpha. https://seekingalpha.com/article/1496612-portfolio-management-10-tips-for-better-results

Tarpley, L. G. (2022, April 5). *8 tips for choosing the best bank*. Business Insider. https://www.businessinsider.com/personal-finance/how-to-choose-a-bank

Taylor, B. (2020, January 16). *Investment strategies to learn before trading*. Investopedia. https://www.investopedia.com/investing/investing-strategies/

TD Canada Trust. (n.d.). *Saving vs. investing: What's the difference?* TD Canada Trust. Retrieved March 27, 2023, from https://www.td.com/ca/en/personal-banking/personal-investing/learn/saving-vs-investing

Town, P. (2017, October 25). *13 investing terms for beginners*. Rule #1 Investing. https://www.ruleoneinvesting.com/blog/how-to-invest/investing-terms/

Turner, T. (2023, March 22). *Investing | what does it mean & how does it work?* Annuity.org. https://www.annuity.org/personal-finance/investing/

Wanderlust Worker. (2016, August 30). *5 reasons why passive income is important*. Wanderlust Worker. https://www.wanderlustworker.com/5-reasons-why-passive-income-is-important/

YFL. (n.d.). *Top 5 reasons why financial literacy is important for youth in 2020*. YFL. https://www.yflfoundation.org/blog/rqngrkko34859ezmheafu09retwkch-batzk-c9zh3

Made in the USA
Las Vegas, NV
14 December 2023

82826846R00095